THE SINGER'S
INSTINCT

ACTIVATE THE 4 IMPULSES THAT UNLEASH THE POWER OF SINGING

By Brandon Brophy

FOREWORD BY DAVE STROUD

THE SINGER'S INSTINCT
A BBVS BOOK / OCT 2012

PUBLISHED BY
BBVS
TORONTO

First Edition
ISBN: 978-0-9880948-0-2

Cover Design by Ryan Howorth and Sean Kosonic
Illustrations by Sean Kosonic
Music Images by Ryan Peplinski and Santiago Ortega
Editing by Anna Ezekiel

ACKNOWLEDGEMENTS

Thanks to Kevin Bonilla, Ryan Luchuck, Dave Stroud, Line Hilton, Michelle Speyer, Carol Bernard, my family, and all my students who illuminated the way for this book.

TABLE OF CONTENTS

Foreword

It was early in the year 1983 and I was in my voice lesson preparing for the state Solo/Ensemble competition. We were working through Mozart's O Isis and Osiris. I had been bitten by the singing bug not too long before this and in the tiny town I grew up in, in Southern Utah, this was the best I was going to get from the available resources. Singing a classical bass/baritone piece was not my idea of cool, but being bitten by the singing bug meant I was going to sing something, even if it was this. The problem was that there wasn't anything out to help me. No real practical singing book or program or internet examples. I had this super nice lady who had studied vocal performance in her youth and a stack of sheet music to pick from. Actually, I wasn't even a real bass/baritone but I also could not figure out how to sing through the higher notes without a break. My voice changed at such an early age (around 13) and the break become obvious from that point on. So, since I could not sing the higher notes and I had no one to really help me figure that out with my voice and no money or resources, I sang O Isis and Osiris. And I sang it a lot!

A few years later I was in college and wanted to start a band. We named it "Educated Guess" and we played all the cool Modern Rock and New Wave cover songs. I struggled. I loved being in the band and I loved music, passionately, but lacking any real practical approach to building my voice my range got smaller and my endurance got shorter the more we played. It was draining the passion out of me.

I began studying a lot with different teachers around the local area. I began to make some progress. I was learning slowly, but at least I was getting somewhere. After a couple of years of studying, I actually began teaching some very beginning students. That is when I really began to learn. Helping others with their voices became the most significant platform for me to learn and I began to open up the top part of my voice. It got very exciting for me. Ironically though, the more I taught and the more my voice grew from this, the more my passion was shifting. Not away from singing, but towards music education. It was the best of both worlds because I was able to sing all day long and teach others what I had learned. My passion to become a rock star faded (yes, I really did want to be a rock star at one point) and my passion for the teaching studio grew. I distinctly remember a rehearsal I was in and I could not get the voice of one of my students out of my head. I kept processing her vocal issues over and over in my mind, trying to come up with an answer, and while it was challenging to come up with answers, it was exciting to process for me. At the end of that rehearsal I knew I was done performing, at least for a while. I threw all my passion into studying, learning, and helping singers everywhere.

Fast forward another 15 or so years and here I am today. I have now worked with some of the most famous singers of the last 2 decades or so. I have worked in recording sessions with many of the top producers and engineers in the industry and toured the world over many times teaching master-classes, private lessons, and training hundreds of teachers. All of this adds up to my first-hand exposure to the need for more and better arts and music education. My passion for teaching has only grown through these amazing experiences, and I see a bigger need for good resources and pipelines of knowledge to flow to singers everywhere. I know my frustrations as a singer could have been fewer if I had had better resources back then. I can also acknowledge that if I had not felt frustrated and singing had come easier, my passion for teaching would have been less, so I am grateful for the adversity I faced.

When Brandon Brophy handed me this book to look over and give feedback, I was excited about what I read. This book would have been the most important book of my youth, had it been available to me back then. Brandon has compiled exactly what I was missing then - a practical approach to developing the singing voice. What you hold in your hands right now may well be what gives you the tools to accomplish those burning dreams you have that will not go away. My advice to you is to read this book and dig into the work it lays out for you. You may have heard the phrase at some point "standing on the shoulders of giants". It means those who accomplish great things do so because of the pathway that others have cleared for them. You could argue that if it were not for Michael Jackson, then Usher, Justin Timberlake, Justin Bieber, Ne-Yo, and many others would not have had so much success. However, each one of those singers put in countless hours of practice and passion into becoming as good as they are. Brandon has created a real world guide for singers to become better and stronger at their craft, but it is up to each one of you to use this book often and practice constantly the tools he has put forward.

I wish you all the best and I know that a lot of hard work is in your future, and I know that just because you have this in your hands means you have already committed yourself to this work. GO DO IT!

Dave Stroud
Sunset Strip, Los Angeles, California
2012

TRACING THE INSTINCT

in·stinct (n-stngkt)
n.
1. An inborn pattern of behavior that is characteristic of a species and is often a response to specific environmental stimuli: the spawning instinct in salmon; altruistic instincts in social animals.
2. A powerful motivation or impulse.
3. An innate capability or aptitude: an instinct for tact and diplomacy.
adj. (n-stngkt)
1. Deeply filled or imbued: words instinct with love.
2. *Obsolete:* Impelled from within.

. . . .

S inging has always been one of the most moving expressions of profound human experiences. The best contemporary singers whose voices move us deeply seem to be so connected to the experience of singing that it is as if singing is a natural extension of their personality. So natural, in fact, that it often leaves the strong impression that one would have to have been born with the voice fully developed in order to sing at all! Even today, the myth that "either you're born with it or you're not" lives on. Why is something that is supposedly natural to us so difficult for most of us to do well? In these pages, you will find many ways to discover that singing indeed is an instinct - one that everybody has, though it will require some effort to properly hone it. If you do the simple work I've laid out, you will be able to unleash it in you.

Singers have been elevated and their songs perfected in modern digital recording studios to such a degree that it makes singing seem untouchable for the rest of us. Worse, reliable, practical information on voice improvement for modern singing is actually rather difficult to find, as the chapter on voice myths near the end of the book makes clear. Many university programs teach singing (most cater to classical music), but only a rare few provide education for teachers interested in voice pedagogy (the study of voice instruction itself). Even these tend to be classically oriented. And even if the instructors on these courses have educational credentials, this certainly doesn't mean they are knowledgeable about balancing voice registers (more on that in the next chapter) in a useful way for modern music. And if that wasn't enough, when the beginning singer eventually figures out that they should learn at least the fundamentals of the language of music in order to improve their singing, where on earth to start with that? Even opening a book on basic music theory is enough to give the novice a heart attack. No wonder singing has received such a reputation as being unattainable!

Still, as neuroscientist Daniel Levitin points out, music powerfully captivates people all over the world, igniting a primordial urge to express and share the human experience in compellingly new and modernly relevant ways - even if it's just in the shower! Singers bring something to the landscape of art that no other artist can - they bring the human story to life in vivid language through words in a powerfully musical way. Importantly, through the singer's individual use of voice and language, the art of singing has the potential to become subtly unique and distinctive to every singer. If the singer is moved by the experience and they are able to channel their experience through their voice in an authentic way, they can create deeply moving and fulfilling expressions of this experience that move us.

> "Music is a means for communicating emotions that we can't convey as well as speech; a metaphor for how we're feeling; it's mental gymnastics for our prediction centers; and it contributes chemically to the strong feelings of being synchronized with our fellow humans."
>
> - DANIEL LEVITIN

On the surface, great vocalists have made singing seem effortlessly easy. But dig a little deeper and you will likely find that in one way or another singers must face many hurdles along a distinctive path of self-discovery.

Discovering your own voice is a process of lost and found. You feel certain pieces missing in your ability to sing as you require, and you embark on the difficult path to find the missing pieces. But when you understand the path that most other singers have walked, you better prepare yourself to recognize critical signs for your own journey.

My story is a typical lost and found story of the singing instinct. It began for me before I remember singing at all. At 8 years old my neighbor would make me play the most difficult left hand parts at her piano. From then on, the spell of music had been cast upon me whenever I sat in front of the keyboard. In later years, my poor grandmother's pleasantly quiet home would have it's silence violently broken during my visits when I would be uncontrollably magnetized to her cabinet piano, igniting whatever musical fireworks came to mind, with my right foot mindlessly planted on the sustain pedal. It wasn't long before the joy of the keyboard extended to singing where the emotional landscapes the music produced gave me release and filled me with a sense of beauty and majestic wonder. Importantly, it gave me channels for unraveling my own experience as a misfiring teenager.

When I turned 15, a soprano from a local conservatory heard me singing and offered me an opportunity to study with her on a limited scholarship. She was very generous to me, and I gained substantially from her wisdom. Yet at the same time, in order to limit any potential strain on my voice, the training I received from her seemed to restrict the expressiveness of my singing by assigning me to an arsenal of classical bass-baritone repertoire, the voice classification that matched my low, undeveloped vocal range at the time. I became depressed with the limited range that I seemed to be stuck with. Singing low, uninteresting songs for the rest of my life, I felt, simply wasn't going to provide a satisfying life in music for me. My voice began to feel strangely disconnected. What I intrinsically gathered from the experience was that the voice I was born with was not cut out for enjoyable singing. While my obsession with music continued, my faith in my voice had been lost. As a result, I felt I had to abandon the world of singing altogether. If I couldn't enjoy singing, I thought, I might as well pursue something I knew I was somewhat good at: I would reluctantly continue my journey as an actor.

Fate had a big surprise in store for me, however. Luckily I had been accepted into a small group of aspiring actors at a university program in Toronto. During my tenure there, the program director decided to experiment with employing a vocal instructor who taught an unusual approach that extended the range of voice by "blending" the upper and lower ranges of the voice together. This, the program director thought, might help make the actors' voices more flexible for characterizations. The method had seen its peak in the '70s and '80s via celebrities in Los Angeles by an influential teacher, Seth Riggs. To my knowledge, this is the only time Mr. Riggs' technique had ever been fully and officially employed at any educational institution in North America. This small twist of fate would revolutionize my understanding of vocal range and put me on a new trajectory that would eventually empower me to fully expand my range far beyond and above the low voice to which I had thought I was limited.

Some years later, I began working intensively with Hollywood coach Dave Stroud who was responsible for creating a revolutionary training methodology for aspiring voice teachers that allowed them to move beyond vague, descriptive voice instruction into direct causational teaching - the principles this book is founded on. Stroud had been CEO and the creative visionary behind Riggs' company for over a decade but had become unable to reconcile many limitations there. This tension between technique and artistic empowerment soon became the impetus for his development of a technology platform that could better service singers. This book is a realization of the same gap that I have repeatedly noticed existing between a singer's technical ability and their ability to be free and expressive in a way that is relevant to our modern culture.

As well as private training, I have also studied music in academia. In my experience of academia, however (although things are slowly changing), the usual standard for training the aspiring

singer is to submerge her deeply in classical music theory or European art music history, or to teach her to adhere to the strict demands of opera and music theatre. This is a wonderful approach for aspiring singers looking for a career in those genres, but how does the student interested in modern music apply this knowledge? The female singer, for instance, simply cannot make do with just the high voice development typically received in classical approaches if she wishes to sing pop or rock songs, which require a strong grasp of the low voice. Even years of operatic training will be difficult for the aspiring rock or R&B singer, female or male, to apply to singing in an authentically modern, liberated way. The question remains: how can you be taught to correctly put your full vocal range to use, free of strain and breaks in a characteristic fashion that is more in line with your own Singer's Instinct and musical culture? We will examine this more closely in the following chapters.

It is not just singing style that has changed, but the culture of modern music itself has evolved massively since the turn of the twentieth century - an entire universe apart from the classical era. Perhaps the biggest shift in modern music has been the collision and fusion in the western continent of African-American culture with North and South American cultures to create a new pallet of vocal and musical colors and rhythms, and a sense of unfiltered authenticity that has profoundly changed what it means to be a singer in the modern world. More than anything else, it is the attention to, and sophisticated, playful use of, rhythmic elements in singing that distinguishes a modern singer from the classical one. This ability to play with rhythm in singing is part of the musical impulse, one of the four impulses we will focus on in this book.

If the aspiring modern singer can manage to get the full range of their voice in shape for modern singing and learn to tap the pulse of modern rhythm, it still doesn't necessarily mean they will have learned how to interpret the music through their voice, via their personality, in a way that is relevant in a contemporary context and fulfilling for them to sing. One can spend years doing an incredible amount of vocal training and yet never arrive at a satisfyingly expressive way of singing. One may never learn the right practicing techniques to fuse these vocal and musical skills to sing with creativity, personality, and instinct.

The definition at the start of this chapter says that an instinct is something we are born with that is characteristic of our species. What could be more instinctual than singing - using your voice to express your experiences? As I will outline shortly,

> "A few strong instincts and a few plain rules suffice us"
>
> - RALPH WALDO EMERSON

anyone can access instinct, singing included. Instinctive singing is not so difficult when you understand some basic vocal and musical laws. The trick is to learn how and where to focus your efforts without losing touch with the enjoyment of it.

Studies have shown that singing provides countless benefits, even if it's in the shower, in the car, at karaoke, or recording songs for your family for special events. Yet it is true that many of us are drawn to singing because we admire from a distance people who rise with acclaim to the international stage. Just don't fall into the trap of believing that successful singing is equal only to a record deal, international travel, and performing to full houses in stadiums. Singing is an art and the music business is only one expression of it.

Yet the desire to hit the world stage can trigger enormous reservoirs of motivation that, if used effectively, can help to propel you there, if that's your desire. You will need the momentum to battle millions of other singers sparring for the one spot on the top of the charts. You'll also need to have exquisite business, networking, personal development, and copious amounts of refined performance skills. But even before any of that, you will have to delve deep into making the art of singing itself distinctively your own.

Without a strong ability to carry a distinctive and competitive singing style, you won't have any commodity to compete for domination of the world stage. And what is the pursuit of recording-artist fame if you're unable to be vocally and musically expressive first? Singing and performing are different skills, related as they may be, and you'll be challenged (and probably harshly criticized) if you attempt to pursue fame or performance acclaim without first having created for yourself a distinctive musical and culturally relevant way of singing. If you aspire to share your personality on the international stage, then the place to start is learning how to musically communicate through your voice, so your personality can shine through in a way that others can enjoy and admire. The start of the grand dream chase is the beginning of rediscovering your singers instinct.

So, for a modern singer who needs a solid place to start on their journey, has lost touch with either their full vocal range or their own sense of style, or is looking to connect with a passionate, authentically modern musical sensibility, we need a more efficient and direct way of accessing that instinct than

> **"Instinct is intelligence incapable of self-consciousness."**
>
> - JOHN STERLING

we've been accustomed to using in the past. If, as the author John Sterling says, instinct is intelligence incapable of self-consciousness, then singers need a way of developing their singing and musicianship skills so these can emerge free of the debilitating weight of self-consciousness to engage with singing in a thrilling and satisfying way.

This book, then, is not about performing or developing the skills needed to succeed in the music industry. Instead, it's about learning to form a meaningful connection to singing - rediscovering the Singer's Instinct. Being an instinctive modern singer means existing at the intersection where your fully developed voice, your understanding of music, your vocal personality, and your ability to practice wisely can mix powerfully together. The more you apply these four skills using the guidelines in this book, the more they will grow into deep impulses, and the stronger, deeper and more alive that intersection can become. When you align with these impulses, you form a deep connection to the Singer's Instinct - an innate creative force that re-ignites a natural, modern expression from within. Only then can your unique relationship to music and your Singer's Instinct fully emerge.

This is not to say that classical singing is off-limits to the experience this book fosters. The method presented in this book is just a direct, accessible way to bring out the Singer's Instinct in you. This book is written for anyone who wants to sing freely and expressively in a contemporarily relevant way. No matter what level of singer you are, this program will guide you through establishing a stronger, more direct connection to your Singer's Instinct: the foundation of what I believe is great singing, shaped not by the pursuit of fame and celebrity status, but motivated from the desire to connect with your instinct for self-expression.

The four impulses of the singers instinct, Voice, Musicality, Personality and Wise Practice, are developed in this book as follows:

The Vocal Impulse: Chapters 1 - 6 will teach you how to tune up your voice for modern singing, supporting you with a healthy vocal technique for your lifelong exploration of modern songs.

The Musical Impulse: Chapters 7 - 11 will initiate you into some of the ideas of modern music for singing, via an exploration of rhythm and techniques to improve your ability to sing in tune.

The Vocal Personality Impulse: Chapters 12 - 15 will encourage you to channel your own personality into your singing, by helping you interpret your songs and apply some basic phrasing techniques.

The Impulse of Wise Practice: Chapters 16 - 20 will lay out some important things to remember as you continue your development.

The purpose of this book is to ignite within you an awakening of your own vocal and musical impulses, driving you directly to an enjoyable singing experience. What matters most with singing, as Whitney Houston says, is that you give singing everything you've got. This book helps you do that.

It is beyond the scope of any book on singing to give you the customized vocal workouts you may need, help you overcome complex individual vocal issues, or allow you to develop vocal virtuosity. Instead, I wish to aid you in the discovery of your instinct for self-expression. In doing so, I have made great attempts to simplify the singing process to make it easier to understand for the beginning and intermediate singer, while still keeping the program accurate, updated, and concise. I hope this will direct you to connect with your own Singer's Instinct in an efficient, practical way.

This book is designed as a compliment to, not a replacement for, your critical voice technique training discipline. By developing and maintaining a strong, healthy voice with a great teacher you improve your chances of being able to draw out the expanses of your Singer's Instinct. Like any book, this program can only provide you with a solid grounding in essential ideas and you should find a teacher to guide you deeper through your unique goals and challenges. Chapter 18 gives some advice on how to find a teacher who can do this. Effective voice training requires a very good vocal teacher who is equipped to assess and balance a wide variety of voices for modern singing. My hope is that by equipping you with the right information, you can avoid the unnecessarily long process I endured. Make sure you get the right help.

And finally, never get discouraged. As you move through the exercises in this book, know that you do not have to get them perfect. In fact, many audiences might tell you that perfect singers are rather boring anyway! Instead, focus on the experiences the exercise is

> "Sing it from your heart, sing it with feeling, and give it everything you've got."
>
> - WHITNEY HOUSTON

trying to create for you, and embrace your mistakes. Make sure you note any changes you feel, even the smallest ones. You will get out of singing at least as much as you put into it, so resist at all costs comparing your growth as an artist to others. Everyone comes into the world of singing with their own strengths and weaknesses and every vocal artist carries within them a powerful and unique story. Remember that your distinctive voice and your story is entirely unique to you and will never be experienced by anyone else ever again. Have fun discovering your own approach to singing, and enjoy exploring what your experience of this fantastic art form will be.

In short, borrow from the strengths of those you admire, but honor your uniqueness. This is your journey. Follow your instincts.

THE VOCAL
IMPULSE

"I don't know what happens to me on stage.
Something else seems to take over."

- MARIA CALLAS

1. THE ABCs OF SINGING

> **Goal:** Understand the 3 core elements of vocal function.
>
> **Why:** These 3 elements form the foundations for this book and they are the only things you can adjust in your voice when you sing. By learning more about these 3 elements, you can create more precise changes in your voice much faster.

. . . .

There are only three elements that you can control to guide your voice into its full potential. I call these the ABCs of singing. When your ABCs are correctly balanced across your whole range, your voice will be flexible and free enough to explore whatever your budding Singer's Instinct impels you to. Your ABCs are:

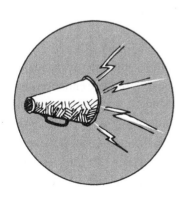

Amplifier Shape: How you adjust the shape of your amplifier, commonly known as your vocal tract, determines vowel shape. It is the space that runs from the edges of your lips to the top of your larynx, commonly known as your voice box, which houses your vocal cords (also known as vocal "folds" - more on that in that in the "C" section below).

Breathing: As you inhale, your vocal cords fully open to allow air to pass through. This causes your lungs to expand, filling with air as they absorb oxygen. When you exhale, the used air in your lungs reverses back up through your trachea (air passage), through your relaxed and open vocal cords, and out your mouth. Your body does this daily without you thinking about it.

Closure of Vocal Cords: You can experience your vocal cords being fully open without any closure when you breath naturally, allowing air to move through them freely. You can experience them fully closed when you hold your breath - no air passes at all. If you say "AH" (as in "father") your vocal cords will maintain just enough closure (not too tight, but not too breathy) to make the sound. This allows some air to pass through, sending them into vibration and creating a basic tone.

How the ABCs Work Together

The tone that is created by the vibration of the vocal cords is amplified and shaped as vowels (the sound "AH" in the example above) mainly via the throat and mouth space above your vocal cords. The entire process happens naturally when we speak and produce words with the whole spectrum of vowels and consonants. Since singing is more sustained than speech, we will likely need more breath than we use in speaking to support the longer lengths of phrases used in singing. Also, higher notes require slightly more air compression, and therefore may also demand more air. Let's examine the ABCs more closely:

Amplifier Shape (Vowels)

Without anything amplifying the sound from your vocal cords, the voice wouldn't be heard much at all. But as we shape the spaces above the vocal cords (our amplifier/vocal tract), we adjust the spaces of the throat (larynx position) and spaces in the mouth (the tongue, jaw, and lips) to amplify and modify that basic sound into what we hear as vowels and consonants. A skilled singer can make small and deliberate adjustments to the subtleties of vowel shapes to better suit higher pitches. This is called vowel tuning - more on this in chapter 5. As well as providing shape and amplification of the sound, vowels also give the overall vocal sound its vibrant and unique tonal color. Although it can take some time to have an awareness of all the parts of your voice, we can usually immediately experience the resonance created by the vowel shaping of our amplifier.

Consider that for every pitch you can make, there are several vowel sounds (between 11 and 20 depending on the accent) that must be coordinated. Furthermore, each vowel you sing creates either low or high voice resonances in differing degrees (more on that in the next chapter).

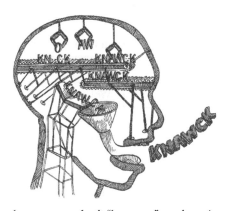

When singing, you want to make sure you don't "hang on" to changing sensations of resonance as you ascend or descend in pitch. If you do you will likely experience a dramatic change for the worse in the way you shape the vowel. You may be inclined to open your mouth wide on high notes, creating the wrong muscular and resonance conditions in the high parts of your vocal range, or to try to drop your larynx low for low notes, creating inefficient vocal cord and resonance patterns in the lower range of your voice. We want to master the correct adjustments of vowel shaping between the low and high voice on every vowel. We will examine this more closely in later chapters.

Looking at the vowel chart on the next page, vowels near the bottom of the chart, such as "AH" and "AA", are termed "low" or "open" vowels, reflecting the low position of the tongue in the mouth as it forms the vowel shape. These vowels engage more easily the low range of the voice and are amplified mainly in the throat. Moving up the chart, the vowels go from open to closed. Vowels such as "OO" and "EE" are called "high" or "closed" vowels and have a high tongue position that more easily engages the high voice. They are amplified mainly in the mouth. Singers who struggle with finding stability and strength in their low voice will require more work with open vowels to engage more of their low voice. People who strain to reach high notes will require more work with closed vowels to more correctly engage their high voice. Vowels are also categorized as "front" and "back" vowels (there are also a few mid vowels such as "UH" which I've included below as a back vowel for simplicity), which reflects the tongue's position from the back to the front of the mouth. These aspects of the vowels can be used for vowel tuning (see chapter 5).

Common North American English Vowels

High	Front Vowels			Back Vowels		
	IPA	Words	Sound	Sound	Words	IPA
	i	beet, neat, geese	EE	OO	boot, noon, goose	u
	I	bit, bin, bill	IH	OH	boat, note, goat	o
	e	bait, nail, gate	AY	EU	book, nook, good	ʊ
	ɛ	bet, net, get	EH	UH	bus, nudge, gust	ʌ
Low Vowels	æ	bat, nap, gap	AA	AH	bought, knock, got	ɑ

Diphthongs

In the above examples, both "AY", as in "bay" ["EH" + "EE"] and "OH", as in "boat" ["OH" + "EU"] can be diphthongs. As with all vowel sounds, the actual sound you produce will vary depending on your dialect. Diphthongs are two adjacent vowel sounds that begins as one and ends as another in the same syllable. Some words with diphthongs include: "I" ["AH"+"EE"], "boat" ["OH"+"EU"], "bow" ["AH"+"EU"], and "out" ["AA"+"EU"]. When a note that is held is a diphthong, some beginning singers give both sounds in a diphthong equal emphasis. Although this is how you would speak a diphthong, because the vowel sounds are held for longer periods in singing doing the same could sound strange or be useful depending on the style you're going for.

In singing, most styles sing on the first part of the diphthong for most of the length that the note is sustained, sliding to the second vowel sound only towards the end of the sustained note, so it is actually barely heard in comparison to the first. Any rule can be broken, however, so you can add contrast to a song by accenting the second part of the diphthong for effect - just don't make it a habit!

Vowels and Larynx Position

High vowels with a high tongue position generally create a lower larynx with increased space in the throat, while low vowels with a low tongue generally have a higher larynx with a smaller space in the throat. Low notes generally require a higher larynx, which means that lower vowels are much easier in a low voice. High notes generally require a lower larynx, so high vowels are much easier in a high voice.

Breathing

When a singer is confronted with the overwhelming emphasis on breathing in many approaches to singing, it might seem as if the only thing a singer can control is their diaphragm (a contracting muscle that is engaged when you take a breath, expanding your lungs and causing them to fill with more air). This can be confusing. The diaphragm itself is an involuntary muscle which you cannot consciously control. But the act of taking a low breath will automatically engage it. A low breath is where your lower lungs expand, causing your belly to inflate outward, as opposed to breathing high into your upper lungs, which causes your chest to rise. A low breath can help get more air supply for longer phrases and help to provide slightly more compression for higher pitches. It can also get more oxygen into your body, helping you to relax your throat and body so your entire vocal mechanism can function more freely - especially in stressful situations like being onstage.

Quite simply, a natural, low breath is often more than sufficient for singing (and according to some vocal experts, although a low breath is ideal, even that isn't completely necessary). It's crucial to note, however, that without the vocal cords closing appropriately and the correct adjustment of the amplifying space for the pitch, attention to breathing alone cannot adjust your voice into the balance it needs for problematic areas of your vocal range. As you will discover in the next chapter, there is much more to a balanced voice than just being relaxed and breathing correctly. However, being aware of your breathing as singers can be helpful to aid in the free vibration of the vocal cords in a relaxed way.

There are many reasons why you may not have a low breath in your daily life. You might feel self-conscious about the size of your midsection, for instance, if you take a deep, low breath. Many people even breathe "backwards": their upper chest rises on the inhale, and the tummy drops out on the exhale. A high breath of this sort can be problematic because only half your lung capacity - your upper chest - is used, causing you to run out of air on longer phrases. It also makes a deep relaxing breath impossible, so you can easily be thrown into a state of hyper mental activity or hyperventilation when you sing.

To find a low breath, you must make sure you don't breath high, into the top of your lungs, but into the lower area of your lungs. You will know you have done this correctly when your relaxed tummy expands with each intake. Your tummy, sides and back should expand outward with your inhale (but do not force them out), and relax back in on the exhale. You should not feel your upper chest rise. An easy way to find a low breath is to be attentive to encouraging the tummy to come inwards as you exhale. You should then feel it drop outwards as you inhale. Another way is to lie down down on your back and allow yourself to relax. Then put your hands on your tummy and notice your breathing: is your tummy moving in and out? You should find that your breathing will naturally drop low into your lungs. See if you can maintain that feeling when standing.

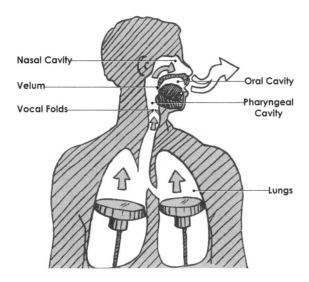

Try to keep your inhalation silent, naturally, through the mouth. Nasal breathing is not recommended as it can drop the soft palate on the inhale, impeding its naturally optimal internal positioning. This will make it difficult, as you shift from inhalation to singing a tone, to start with a correct vowel formation.

Closure of Vocal Cords

Your vocal cords are the source of your vocal tone and are extraordinarily miniature compared to other musical instruments. They range anywhere between ½" - 1" (1 - 2.5 cm) long, roughly the length of a fingernail! The cords are a pair of muscles and tissue that lie flat inside your larynx (voice-box). The larynx hangs over your air passage (trachea) about halfway down the throat. The front aspect shows itself in most men as a prominent protrusion and is known in lay terms as the "Adam's apple", though women can also feel theirs with less prominence. The higher voices of women are the result of their generally shorter vocal cord lengths compared to men.

Larynx (Voice Box)

Epiglottis

Vocal Cords

Superior (top) view

There will be times when you will discover that you seem to be lacking adequate breath to support a note. In this situation, don't make the dangerous assumption that you simply need more air, or that you must support the vocal cords by increasing breath pressure. In the overwhelming majority of cases, it is likely that the vocal cords are closing too hard or aggressively, causing them to swell slightly so that they cannot close in an efficient way for the note you are singing.

The reverse is also possible (and common): the closure of the vocal cords may not be strong enough and/or the cords may not be holding together firmly enough, causing you to lose valuable air. In both these cases, you will require an adjustment of the amount of closure by the vocal cords themselves, and that will require that you lessen the breath pressure until you find the appropriate balance. When a balance of vocal cord closure is achieved, you will naturally and correctly apply the right amount of breath pressure that your vocal cords require. Although the increasing and decreasing closure of the vocal cords will create increasing and decreasing amounts of breath pressure on its own, you will still likely experience the need for less breath, rarely more.

If you are singing with optimal vocal cord closure but still discover that you are short of breath to finish a long held note, then the answer is fortunately rather simple: find a deeper breath before the beginning of the phrase with the note, or simply break up the sung phrase to find a place to breathe closer to the held note.

But why does there tend to be so much focus on breathing in the singing community? The answer to this conundrum, I believe, is that singers and teachers whose voices are well adept at shifting easily throughout the range hardly experience conscious changes of their amplifier shape or the necessary changes in the efficient vibration of the vocal cords much at all, as the correct patterns become deeply ingrained.

Therefore, many teachers and highly experienced singers may find that the only part of the singing mechanism that they can dramatically feel is the action of the abdominal wall pressing air out of the lungs and against the vocal cords, providing them with compressed air. For them, it becomes the part of the singing mechanism that is most dominantly seen (with the belly expanding and contracting) and felt during vocalization. Also, many female vocalists trained in a classical manner sing with a breathier tone in their lower range much more often than do modern singers, requiring significantly more airflow. It is likely that it is for these reasons that the emphasis on breath control is often overestimated in the world of singing.

> "The overestimation of breath support at the cost of the glottis (the airspace between the vocal folds) and vocal tract (the airway between the glottis and the mouth) is a typical mistake of beginners (both singers AND teachers). This is dangerous because breath pressure is by far the most powerful part [of the vocal mechanism]."
>
> - DR. HUBERT NOE

Because most modern singers use microphones, they no longer need to train their voices to produce the maximum amount of sound possible for a long period to time to fill an auditorium without a microphone - as is the case with operatic singing. While slightly increasing air pressure does provide more intensity in a balanced voice, the vocal cords and correct amplifier adjustments must be trained to balance that increase. But in the beginning, powerful breath pressure is just not necessary for a voice that hasn't developed basic vocal coordinations of shifting through its range efficiently. As you will learn later, vocal power is gained in another, much more efficient way.

Now that you have a good grasp of the 3 basic elements of singing, in the next chapter we will look at how the voice can be used as a musical instrument.

EXERCISES

1) Where are your vocal cords located?

_____

2) Roughly how long are your vocal cords?

_____

3) Put your hand on your tummy as you take a breath in. Do you notice your tummy expand as you take a breath, or does your ribcage rise instead?

_____

4) Lie down and see if you can feel your breath drop naturally into your lower lungs. Can you can maintain that feeling as you stand?

_____

2. YOUR VOICE AS AN INSTRUMENT

Goal: Understand how your voice makes musical sounds on a basic level.

Why: Your voice is your musical instrument, and you should understand how your instrument works so you can develop your voice for singing. Your vocal cords and the size and quality of your resonating areas are the one-of-a-kind vehicle through which all your expression and creativity will flow.

. . . .

N ow that you have a basic understanding of how the voice works, it's time to explore what happens when we try and use it as a musical instrument. Perhaps what makes the voice most challenging in this regard is the dramatically shifting sensations we experience as we sing throughout our range. The most distinct sensations we feel are those of voice registers. If you want to learn how to sing in a healthy way and discover your natural voice, you will need to understand how to sing in a balanced, natural way throughout all of your voice registers.

A voice register is an area of the vocal range where a series of notes is experienced in a similar way: each register will require slightly different actions of your vocal cords, and will resonate in a slightly different way in your body. Because of this, the sensations of registers are subjective, varying from person to person and particularly from one musical style to another. Singing in a rock style will have slightly different register considerations than opera, for instance.

There are a number of registers in a fully developed vocal range. These can include chest, upper chest, middle, head, super-head, and whistle registers. Although you should ultimately learn how to healthily access even the extreme notes in your range, for efficiency in this program we will

> **"My voice technique is chest voice, head voice, and singing back and forth between them."**
>
> - BOBBY MCFERRIN

focus exclusively on only the first four registers.: the chest, upper chest, middle, and head registers. I will mostly refer to the lower registers of the chest and upper chest as the "low voice", and to the upper registers such as middle and head as the "high voice".

Low Voice

If you put your hand on your chest as you speak, or if you sing in the low range of your voice correctly (without a breathy tone), you will most likely feel your voice resonate almost entirely in your chest cavities. The deep, full, somewhat heavy-feeling low voice, usually referred to as the chest voice, can be found by speaking vowels like "AH" (as in "father") and "AA" (as in "bat").

To create the slower vibrations of the low voice, the thyroarytenoid muscles (TA) in the vocal cords create shorter cords with less tension. Many instruments get their lower ranges from longer strings, but the vocal cords make up for the difference of their shorter vocal cords by loosening the tension in the vocal cords, thereby creating lower pitches. The sound from the low voice is amplified and gets its power mainly from the bigger resonant spaces in the throat.

High Voice

When singing in the high voice (commonly referred to as the "head register"), many singers feel the sound resonate almost entirely in their head. If you keep your hand on your chest but then say "WEE" (as in "week") in a gentle, high voice as if you were spurring on the playfulness of a child, you probably won't feel your voice resonate much at all in your chest. You can also try saying "WOO" up in your head voice as if you were shouting out in excitement at a sports match. Both give sensations of head voice in our everyday lives. The light, thin and empty feeling head voice can also be found using vowels like "OO" (as in "boot") and "EE" (as in "beet").

To create the faster vibrations of the high voice, the cricothyroid muscles (CT) are the most active, creating longer vocal cords with increased tension. This creates the increased vibration speeds required for higher pitches. The higher pitches of the high voice are amplified mainly by the smaller resonant spaces in your mouth.

Your Comfort Zone

One vocal challenge limits nearly all of a singer's abilities in modern singing: the heavy low voice and the light feeling high voice are vastly different experiences to the beginning singer. We usually feel comfortable with only one and very uncomfortable with the other, causing us to experience great difficulty when trying to sing between the upper and lower voice. If you are only comfortable with one register, it will greatly limit your range and therefore your expressive capacity will also be limited. Great singing is about being comfortable with both and being able to shift easily between them!

The Singer's Critical Bridge

The reason this is so difficult is because the human voice makes its most dramatic and significant transition of sensation, or most critical bridge, between the low and the high voice. If coordinated correctly, this transition happens between between the notes Eb4 and F4 (just above middle C on the piano) for most men, and around Ab4 and Bb4 for women. Some men and women with heavier, deeper voices may experience this change slightly lower in their ranges, or slightly higher in their ranges if their voices are lighter. To maintain an even voice, the change in sound and pitch requires gradual shifts in two ways:

1. Changing dominant amplifier: The spaces that are responsible for providing the biggest amplification of the pitches you sing also shifts from the throat in the low voice to the mouth for the high voice. So in order to transition through the critical bridge evenly in either direction, you must make sure you don't "hang-on" to the amplifier alignment associated with either the low or high voice that is most familiar to you. It needs to gradually change to the other as you sing in either direction for the voice to continue to work efficiently.

 2. Changing musculature of vocal cords: The thyroarytenoid muscles (TA) that are primarily responsible for producing the lower voice hands over to the cricothyroid muscles (CT) which primarily produces the upper voice. For a fully developed range, however, both must be trained to work in an antagonistic and regulated balance with the other.

As Titze notes, trained singers are able to balance both muscles without overusing either one. Untrained singers on the other hand are inclined to use either all of one muscle, and none of the other, causing the more familiar muscle coordination to over-work too high or low in the range creating vocal strain and other imbalances.

The Singer's Most Essential Skill

The most important skill to learn in singing is how to shift between the low and high voices smoothly and easily.

> "A number of muscle activation studies conclude that speakers and singers - particularly trained vocalists - tend to balance CT and TA muscle activity, utilizing neither to its maximum potential. Researchers theorize that humans naturally are inclined to use all or none of a particular muscle. Training can help vocalists use just part of a particular laryngeal muscle's capability."
>
> - INGO TITZE

The Interaction of the ABCs Across Your Range

 Amplifier: The vocal cords in the larynx themselves produce only a small buzzing sound. It's the two long narrow tubes of spaces of the throat and mouth above the larynx that amplifies that basic tone creating vowels, consonants, and giving us our unique tonal qualities. But these two amplifying spaces also have one more important function.

As the vibration speeds that your vocal cords make must increase more and more for higher pitches, they need support in order to continue to function efficiently. When you optimally shape your vowels, they align with certain harmonics that are from the basic pitch and provide an even bigger boost in sound (called the "sweet spot" - more on that in chapter 5). This alignment creates acoustic energy that presses down over the larynx, countering the breath pressure from your lungs, and supporting the ability of the vocal cords to vibrate even more efficiently. This energy is called acoustic back pressure. It creates even more sound generating a cyclical loop of intensifying energy.

How you adjust your amplifier (vowel shape) should change slightly depending on where you are in your range, and the conventions of the kind of music you are singing. The throat space is often the most important and problematic one. This is because the larynx is most often too high in the high voice, limiting the resonant capacity of the mouth space thereby creating vocal imbalances.

 Breathing: Research has shown that the lungs are capable of providing 100 times more air pressure than the vocal cords can handle. Rarely should you use more air to reach a pitch, especially if you feel like you are straining. Too much air from your lungs can overwhelm the delicate vocal cords and cause them to close tightly if air is blasted too rigorously.

Closure of vocal cords: Since both muscles (TA & CT) should be active in a full range, the CT muscles may dominate in the higher ranges, but will still need the antagonistic flex of the TA muscles as well to keep the voice from going breathy, or "flipping" into falsetto (more below). The reverse is true in the low voice.

Falsetto

In 1986, Prince released his single "Kiss" that exploded across the international billboard charts winning him a Grammy for the best R&B performance and eventually ranking among the top 150 singles of all time. A big part of what made this song distinctive was the unique way in which he used falsetto. Although a peculiar sounding tone, falsetto is relatively easy to sing in, so many singers have used it to compliment their distinctive sound. Artists such as The Bee-Gee's, The Darkness, Scissor Sisters, Elton John, Franki Valli, Sarah McLachlan, Whitney Houston, and many others have all borrowed from it's unique sound.

If you don't adjust your amplifier (vowel shape) from your lyrics in the optimal fashion, the vocal cords won't get the acoustic energy from the amplifier that they need to support their function. The vocal cords will lose their ability to stay closed, causing your voice to go into a breathy, falsetto-like tone. When you are unable to pass from the lower to the upper voice smoothly, or vice versa, the voice breaks, cracks, strains, creates a breathy tone, or any number of other more serious problems.

Falsetto can either indicate a defect in an unbalanced voice, or it can be used as an expressive vocal effect. It occurs when the TA muscles that are dominant in the low voice give way completely in the upper registers, leaving only the CT muscles to maintain tension, which is insufficient to maintain a full sounding, balanced voice in the upper ranges. Remember, both the CT and TA muscles work together across the whole range in a balanced voice. In falsetto, the vocal cords "pop" apart, creating a crack, break, or a sudden breathy or airy tone along with a peculiar sounding tonal quality, as only the outer edges of the vocal cords vibrate. Most presence is lost from the voice, making it very ineffectual for singing in general, although many singers, inluding Prince as mentioned above, have developed their falsetto to be a hallmark of their unique sound. Because this produces an interesting and expressive vocal effect, many singers use it to convey emotion in a particular way, and for that it can be very powerful. However, the peculiar tone and dramatic break it creates in your voice doesn't allow for an even sounding and feeling voice and isn't a means for singing high notes with a natural sounding full tone. Although falsetto can really support a person's unique vocal style, in the beginning of voice training it should generally be avoided unless it is being used to find a sense of ease and release in the high voice, or to create an effect. The most important thing you can learn as a vocalist is the ability to sing from one register to another, by allowing the feelings of resonance to shift easily, without strain and without going into falsetto on all vowels. We will examine this more closely in the next chapter.

Women vs Men

Men tend to have longer and thicker vocal cords than women, which means men generally experience a wider low range while women experience a more extended upper range. Men experience their critical bridge in their voice about half an octave lower than women, but both experience their low and high voices, and their critical bridge, in a similar way. Because the male voice has more vocal cord "weight", it can make transitioning at the critical bridge more difficult than for women, as the extra weight makes the change of sensation much more dramatic.

Children vs Adults

The function of the vocal cords for both girls and pre-puberty boys is the same as for women - the only difference is that a woman's voice usually deepens slightly without necessarily dropping in pitch like it does for men. However, when a boy hits puberty, his larynx undergoes a massive change and he can suddenly find his voice dropping up and down in pitch as it struggles to find some continuity from the previous, young voice.

EXERCISES

1) What is the difference between falsetto and a full high or head voice?

_____

_____

2) Approximately what range of notes form your critical bridge?

_____

3) Try saying "AH" in a strong, spoken voice in your lower range. Does it feel strange or familiar to you?

_____

4) Sing a low note in a similar way to how you might speak it. Do the vocal cords lose their ability to stay closed when you try to sing?

_____

5) Say "WEE" in a light, airy falsetto voice into your upper range, free of strain. How easily can you experience your high voice?

_____

6) Sing a high note in a similar way to how you spoke it above. Do the vocal cords lose their ability to stay closed? Do you find that the vocal cords become too tight?

_____

3. YOUR VOICE-HABIT

Goals: Understand how to identify your voice-habit and how it affects the development of essential singing skills.

Why? Your voice is an instrument like any other – except it's much more fussy than other instruments! If you understand your voice-habit, you will be better equipped to deal with its surprises so you can keep your Singer's Instinct flowing.

. . . .

In 2011, I worked with a prominent R&B artist who had been experiencing some fatigue in the recording studio. He had quite the gift already for soaring melodies and intricate melismatic vocal runs, but his producers were worried his voice was tiring too quickly. They wanted him to get help.

As we began working through his voice, I could hear strain and a break at the top of his middle register. Above that, he would typically sing in a breathy, airy tone for his high notes.

Diagnosing him quickly as a "strainer", I went to work taking the pressure off his voice mid-way up his range. This allowed him to sing more easily into his high voice with fullness without going into falsetto. "Do you feel the difference between that strong, free voice in your higher range you have now, and the falsetto you were doing before?" I asked him. "I'm not sure," he replied. "Something definitely feels different". So

I asked him to demonstrate both the falsetto and full head voice sound, which he could by then do with ease. "Wow", he replied. "I can really feel alot more strength and control in my upper range ."

The next day, I received a text from his producer. "I don't know what you did to his voice," he said, "but he is singing like crazy now. It's amazing!"

From that point forward, the singer's recordings had powerful, full and rich high notes in a voice that had continuity with no breaks. Because his voice was able to stay even from bottom to top, he grew even more confident in the studio and onstage. There was no longer the distinctive crack he had been experiencing in his voice, and he was no longer tiring from his studio work. He has since become a very influential international R&B singer.

This experience of having a divided range while singing happens to many of us as beginning singers. As a singer, when you ascend or descend in pitch, you feel shifts in resonance from one part of your body into another. The most significant and problematic shifting usually occurs from the low into the high voice and/or vice versa. Most often, when you have to sing a melody that moves from one area of your voice into another, the voice quickly becomes unstable, and you may find your voice uncontrollably breaking or singing with a breathy tone, often producing a falsetto coordination. A connected voice, then, is balanced from one register into another without any of these breaks. This is the most important skill you can learn as a vocalist.

Voice-Habits

Nearly anyone with experience trying to sing consistently and correctly on pitch quickly learns that there are certain notes within their voice that seem easier and some that seem much harder to sing on pitch, never mind singing the notes in any way close to what they intended. These difficult areas usually occur in bridge areas of the voice, particularly the critical bridge. If you don't find a balanced way through those awkward notes, the wear and tear of your singing experience can accumulate quickly, becoming extremely taxing on the muscles in your throat and your vocal cords. The particular manner in which you struggle is your voice-habit.

It's important to remember that virtually every singer that has ever existed, from professional to amateur, has probably struggled to some degree with at least one of these habits. That means that you should not expect perfection - especially too soon. You do not need to have mastered your voice-habit, or have a fully developed voice, to enjoy singing! Instead of regarding them as completely negative, use the habits as a guide to help inform, simplify and focus how you practice your singing. Later in the program, we  will look at how these habits can be used for the development of a unique style. But it's also important to note that if you experience difficulties reaching common pitches anywhere throughout your range, singing can potentially wear down the health of your voice. Over time, your technical and expressive abilities will gradually diminish further, and you will lack vocal strength, range, ease, endurance and stamina. In extreme cases, you also risk developing severe vocal issues from misuse, which can permanently damage your voice. So it's important to ensure you are able to establish some way of singing in a balanced manner, without being boxed in to the limitations of your voice-habit.

In the beginning, most singers have trouble singing easily through their critical bridge, the transitional area between your low and high voice. To properly shift between these registers, the singer must learn how to allow the sensations of one register to shift in a balanced way into the next register. What's more, the singer must learn to do this on every vowel used in their dialect. Certain vowel sounds will be more difficult than others depending on the voice-habit of the singer. Different singers may experience this in slightly different ways, so it's important that you learn what it feels like for you using tools that are appropriate for your voice-habit.

Remember: As singers, you may feel awkward changes of resonance, but a listener will not hear the shifting resonant sensations that we feel to the same degree; they will just perceive an even, free-sounding voice.

There are four common voice habits, one of which you usually get stuck in as you seek to balance and strengthen your voice. Understanding which one you get stuck in is important to understanding how to improve your vocal skills quickly. Then you can learn which tools are most helpful for treating your voice habit. Although we want to have a means of expanding your vocal ability beyond your habit, be careful not to regard the your habits as entirely negative as all the habits can be used to explore and develop your own unique singing style (which you will do in the vocal personality section, the third Singer's Instinct impulse). However, you should be aware that as your voice develops, your voice-habit may change and, as it does, you will need to use different tools to improve. Identifying which voice-habit you usually get stuck in requires a personal assessment of your voice by an experienced teacher trained in identifying and balancing voice-habits.

1. The Strainer

Many of us really enjoy John Mayer's passionate delivery through his distinctive bluesy voice, full of richness and color. We love his voice, and most of us wouldn't expect any more out of him than what he gives us in spades! If were to look closely at his voice, we might be surprised to learn that he doesn't really use much of his upper voice at all. In fact, in his popular song "Waiting On The World To Change", for example, it seems like he is straining his voice trying to reach the highest notes, which aren't even particularly high when compared to other popular male songs. We don't pay much attention to that, and rightly so, because his delivery is so authentic and enjoyable. The disadvantage of his approach is that we may never be able to experience his upper range in his singing. Why does John Mayer experience this limited range?

This type of singer is most comfortable in the low voice of their speaking range, but tends to carry too much of the feeling of the low voice too high through the critical bridge into their high voice. A strainer has overdeveloped thyroarytenoid (TA) muscles, while the muscles that governs the head voice are underdeveloped, or not developed at all. As such, strainers are also most familiar with the voice as amplified from the throat, but usually don't know how to hand over the dominant amplification to the mouth for the upper voice, especially through their critical bridge.

The ABCs of the strainer: This singer is unable to let go of the throat as the primary amplifier as the pitches ascend through their critical bridge. As the strainer tries to sing higher through this area, the throat amplifier must get smaller to resonate the increasingly higher frequencies. So the larynx in the throat must rise higher and higher to create this smaller space.

But the larynx can only rise so much before it reaches a limit and cannot continue to amplify higher frequencies. The muscles in the throat then become increasingly tense as the singer "hangs on". The singer will experience strain, increased volume on high notes, and/or harsh sounds, sudden breathiness, and/or their high notes may be flat (under the intended pitch) with the words and vowels sounding distorted. The voice may tire quickly, but more crucially this voice-habit can create serious problems, such as vocal nodules, if it is not correctly addressed.

Goal: To experience transitioning out of your low voice, engage and strengthen the muscle and amplifier coordinations that govern your higher registers, and learn to balance the low and the high voice with ease, without going into falsetto or strain. We examine many ways to do this in the next chapter.

2. The "Light" Singer

This type of singer is often most comfortable singing in a very light, often breathy tone, with the vocal cords working only lightly. The effect is that they may seem to carry the feeling of their high voice too low in their vocal range.

It is possible to sing in this way across the vocal range without too much difficulty; however, the voice may lack naturalness, fullness, stability, and strength, causing your lower and mid-range to be limited in dynamics. This singer may also find themselves continuously out of breath as the vocal cords cannot close fully.

The ABCs of the light singer: This singer is unable to let go of the mouth as the primary amplifier when they sing in their low voice. While the mouth amplifier is able to create much smaller spaces for higher frequencies in the high voice, it can't provide the bigger space required for amplification of the lower frequencies in the low voice. This means that the vocal cords also do not get the crucial energy they need to vibrate efficiently on the low notes.

This singer also becomes reliant on the CT muscles of the high voice, and does not know how to correctly use the TA muscles of the low voice. Without your vocal cords working strongly enough, particularly in your low range, your voice can take on a breathy tone, or even a somewhat peculiar sounding quality in the context of modern music. So this type of singer often experiences loss of airflow and may find themselves often short of breath and tiring quickly.

It's crucial to remember that though this singer may appear to need more breath control, they really need to learn to correctly access their low voice to gain the correct balance of the vocal cords so they use less air, rather than more.

Goal: To experience the low area of the voice in a strong, spoken quality, without excessive airflow, and to transition from the low to the high voice without strain, breathiness or going into falsetto.

3. The Flipper

This type of singer has a fully functioning and stable low voice, but rather than carrying the feeling of the low voice too high, creating tension, as does the strainer, flippers don't strain much at all. Rather, they completely "let go" of their vocal cords when ascending from their low to high voice, creating a break, leaving their high voice in weak sounding and breathy-toned falsetto coordination.

Many singers falsely believe they belong to this voice-habit because they experience a break in their voice. However, although this singer is anchored in the feeling of the low voice (unlike the light voice-habit). they experience virtually no strain (unlike the strained voice-habit),

There is a distinct break between the flipper's low and high voices where their voice suddenly creates a breathy tone, and a big shift in the quality of the voice. They are unable to produce an even, strong sound in their upper voice. Before you make the assumption that you are flipper, ask yourself if you are anchored in your low voice, straining just before your voice breaks. If so, you are most likely a strainer.

The ABCs of the flipper: This singer is able to maintain the correct amplifier conditions of the low and high voice, but there is a distinctive break in the tonal qualities between them.

The primary issue is that they are unable to maintain the correct coordination of both the TA and CT muscles working together through the critical bridge and into the high voice. The TA muscles let go entirely at the bridge, and the CT muscles alone doesn't have the antagonistic pull it needs from the TA to maintain the even tension it needs for the higher voice.

Goal: To sing evenly from the low to the high part of the voice without straining, breaking or going into falsetto.

4. The Balanced Voice

The type of singer who can easily shift between their low and high voice through their critical bridge is less common, but it does occur and it ought to be your ultimate goal. Balanced habits sing evenly with a good degree of strength from the low to the high parts of their range with no strain, breaks, or unintentional breathiness, in a natural manner similar to some of the modern singers mentioned at the beginning of this chapter.

The ABCs of the balanced voice: This singer is able to smoothly and gradually hand over the dominant amplification from the throat to the mouth when ascending (and vice versa descending). Because amplification is constant from the low to high voice, they receive back pressure support from above the larynx throughout the whole range, and use the correct amount of breath support from below the larynx without blowing too much air, or applying too much breath pressure. They are also able to balance the functionality of both the TA muscle of the low voice and the TA muscle of the high voice together without overusing either one at any point in the range.

NOTE: Quite commonly, singers and even voice teachers may believe they are balanced simply because they experience gentleness on both their low and high notes. However, many undeveloped or classically trained singers have little vocal cord strength in the lower parts of the range because they are not fully engaging the TA muscles that governs the lower voice. It is true that avoiding the fullness of the low voice can save the singer from straining on notes in the middle register or higher. However, having a light approach is often inadequate when singing modern songs because the singer can't match the strength in the lower ranges of modern singers. In these cases, they should train their voices as the light voice habit.

EXERCISES

1) The things I most want to improve about my voice are:

_____

_____

2) My voice-habit is:

_____

3) The voice (low/high) I am most comfortable with is:

_____

4) The area I need the most help in familiarizing/balancing is:

_____

5) My goal, as is appropriate for my voice-habit, is to:

_____

_____

4. OVERCOMING YOUR VOICE-HABIT

Goals: Learn to use the most common tools for improving your voice-habit.

Why? Singing songs can be difficult for a number of reasons, including changing pitches, rhythmic variations, emotion, and, most importantly, vowel changes within difficult areas of the voice. Prioritizing your development to maintain the fullest range possible according to your voice-habit is the most focussed way to learn.

· · · · · · · · · ·

I n earlier chapters, we discussed how the voice differs from other instruments and how it can be difficult to navigate properly. This is because the voice has registers that feel and function very differently from each other - the most dramatic and important changes taking place between the low and high voice. It's important to allow these registers to shift smoothly when singing your songs, and to remember how to  muscularly disengage your strongest register and engage or encourage the register you are most challenged by.

Resistance to changing registers is the root of virtually all of a singer's technical difficulties. Try not to fight it. Remember, there is an entire language of vowels and consonant combinations that you will have to sing with, and many of those can be difficult in different voice registers. All of them must eventually be coordinated with a good degree of ease on all of the pitches in your vocal registration if you want to experience ease in your singing.

Staying Tuned Up

Many singers experience the greatest difficulty between the voice registers within the bridge areas because they tend to want to reach with the feeling of one register into another, either up or down. By far the most difficult and problematic bridge area is the critical bridge, where singers try to carry the feeling of the low voice into the high voice, or vice versa, with both the musculature and the amplifiers (throat and mouth) that govern the low or high voice. This creates vocal strain and distorts optimal vowel sounds. If the optimal vowel formation is not maintained in these areas, the voice quickly becomes imbalanced, which can spiral a singer's voice into strain and a host of other problems.

The challenge is to make sure you can transition evenly between the low and high voice with fullness and ease. The high voice may feel much lighter and more insecure than the lower part of your voice, which may feel heavier and more bras. However, these internal sensations do not reflect what your voice actually sounds like. Every singer experiences a balanced voice in slightly different ways, so you need to learn what it feels like for you.

Tip 1: The secret is to allow the sensations of one register to shift evenly into the next register. You must become familiar with, learn to accept, and ultimately become unresisting to these changing sensations in order to master them!

Tip 2: Stick to exercises for most of your practicing routines rather than singing actual songs until you have a good grasp of how to sing through most vowel sounds easily through your critical bridge.

Tip 3: Practice all your exercises with an easy dynamic - that is, not too loud or too quiet.

Tip 4: Find a "home" exercise and adapt it as you improve. A home exercise is one that you feel most comfortable in and that you can return to if things get out of balance or too confusing.

In the beginning, to learn to sing easily between the different parts of your range, you need to:

1. Identify which voice-habit you have,

2. Use tools and sounds that help you balance your habit,

3. Avoid sounds that draw you back into your old habit until your voice is stronger and more balanced.

---

1. The Strainer

The strainer is by far the most common and problematic voice-habit for singers. This kind of vocal tension may be interesting to some as a vocal effect; however, vocal strain is viciously damaging and creates a downward spiral into vocal damage that can end your ability to sing.

For the strainer it can be very difficult to allow the lighter-feeling, headier aspect of the voice to properly engage in words and notes that are in the critical bridge or the high voice, especially on words with wide vowels like "AA", "AH", etc. The result is that you may sing with too much feeling of the low voice and strain with those words. Vocal strain interferes with optimal vowel formation when singing. It either engages too high a larynx or locks the tongue in the wrong position in the mouth for the pitch, which triggers the vocal mechanism to tighten.

An uncontrollably high larynx is the main source of body tension for singers and is the most common and problematic vocal problem of all. It is the root cause of a whole series of other inconvenient (to say the least) problems such as nasality, breathiness, lack of breath support or strength, imprecise pitches (frequently missing the note you intend to sing), fatigue, lack of control, tonal imbalances... the list goes on. Singing consistently with an uncontrollably high larynx can also result in a number of long term vocal issues which can potentially scar the voice for good and limit the expressiveness of your singing.

TIP: To see if your voice-box rises, you can monitor its movement by lightly keeping your finger on the tip of your Adam's apple (this is not as prominent in women, but you can still feel its movement by touching it).

Although singing with strain is common and even a part of some vocal styles, it is nevertheless important to recognize if the urge to shout or to sing powerfully without optimal vowel alignment (more on that in the next chapter) is frequent for you. This can occur especially when you are performing with a loud band with bad monitoring, and/or you are not able to hear your own voice well. Because the high voice isn't felt as powerfully by the singer as the low voice, many singers onstage fall prey to the belief that they are not being heard when singing correctly in their high voice. Remember, the voice needs to transition efficiently between the low and high voice in order to work freely. All it takes is one wrong vocal move of pushing, shouting, flipping into falsetto, or mistakenly going into a breathy tone for a domino effect of further wrong moves to occur which can quickly wipe out the feeling of ease in your voice and vocal balance!

There are many factors that can contribute to vocal strain. Because it occurs in so many ways, it often requires a number of different solutions depending on the exact nature of the problem and the ideal of the singer. Here are some commonly effective solutions for the strainer voice-habit to be to applied in the order given:

1. Accept shifting, "weaker" sensations on higher ranges: Allow the sensations to shift away from your low voice gently, even allowing your voice to be slightly breathy to lesson the grab of the chest muscle, and allow the shift into your high voice, ideally maintaining a balance without the voice breaking or straining.

2. Familiarize yourself with falsetto: If you're completely new to your high voice, allow yourself to sing in a gentle falsetto temporarily to get used to the sensation of using the new CT muscle. Once you get comfortable with that, aim to maintain a balanced voice, without letting your vocal cords come apart as you transition into your high voice.

3. Resist increasing volume on high notes: Think getting louder on higher notes is going to help you reach them with less strain? It won't. It's only going to make it worse by causing your vocal cords to tighten more to resist the extra air. Make sure you don't increase the volume past an easy dynamic (not too loud or breathy), especially on high notes. Try being gentler, and learn to establish the right balance before attempting louder intensities and volumes.

4. Use less air: Pronounce the consonants more strongly, or use a cry or a whimper as you sing your exercises. This can help lessen the amount of vocal cord being used causing you to require less air to vibrate them effectively. Be extremely attentive to getting louder or blasting more air on high notes - make sure you diminuendo and use less air (but not overly breathy or falsetto) on higher pitches until your coordination improves.

5. Be gentle with consonants: Use consonants such as "b" and "m" before your vowels as assistance for the vocal cords in establishing moderate airflow. Some singers may experience tightness or a squeeze in their critical bridge area, in which case they may experiment with finding greater ease by removing consonants with their vocal work entirely. If your voice begins to struggle again, however, be sure to add the consonants back in again.

6. Choose scale patterns and starting pitches wisely: Use scale patterns with notes that are spread apart rather than close together, and start with high notes in the scales that are just above your critical bridge. Gradually sing the scales with incrementally lower and higher keys. This will help to reduce the habit of reaching from area of the voice into another. Use descending one octave scale patterns, as in the examples given on the next page, starting just into your high voice above the critical bridge, working the voice downward through the transition. Repeat on narrow vowels and lighter consonants such as "WEE" ("weak"), "BOO" ("boot"), "BAY", "BOH" ("boat").

You can also use longer scale patterns of more than an octave.

7. Vowel sounds to avoid in the beginning: Avoid anything that encourages more of the low voice rather than less, making your higher notes difficult to experience with ease. You may wish to avoid "AH", "AA", and hard consonants such as "g" and "k" unless advised by an expert in voice registration. Also avoid short scale patterns such as the 5-tone or semi-tone scale, as they will likely increase the engagement of the low voice, rather than diminish it as is necessary for improving this voice-habit.

8. Order of vowel work: Progress through work with every vowel sound, ideally in the following order, trying to maintain the spoken-ease of vowel production from one vowel into the next: EE/OO/OH/EU/UH/AY/IH/EH/AA/AH. If you experience strain, return to the previous vowel to re-establish a sense of ease in the voice.

9. Practice in front of a mirror: Make sure your lips don't pull back into a smile with words or vowels, especially on high notes. This is particularly common with the front vowels (EE, IH, AY, EH, AA) because the higher resonances are more apt to encourage the larynx to rise. If you notice yourself doing this, stick your lips out so they're rounded on any high notes that are giving you problems so that you sing the vowel through "OO" lips. This increases the space throughout your vocal tract (your mouth and throat), which helps to drop your larynx. Eventually, however, you should aim to allow the lips to return to a more neutral position after you tune your voice into the correct resonances.

10. Use a dumb sound: Temporarily practice singing your vocal exercises using an exaggerated "dumb" sound (like yogi the bear). This allows the larynx to stay low on high notes. After you master that, try and maintain the lower larynx position, without the exaggerated sound.

The resulting sound shouldn't be dumb-sounding, breathy, or strained. Check your larynx position in a mirror or with your finger to make sure it's not too high.

11. Be aware of inappropriate tension: As a vocalist, you must be extremely attentive to any inappropriate build-up of tension in the body, especially in the throat. If this occurs, it's possible that your larynx is still too high and you may need to exaggerate further the previous exercise. Tension may also gather in the tongue or jaw. Resting your palms on the jaw line can sometimes be enough to allow these mechanisms to better adjust.

The remainder of these suggestions are for use in the actual singing of lyrics in songs.

12. Use one sound in place of the lyrics: A good way to get started with all your songs is to remove the lyrics entirely and sing the melody on a sound that is comfortable for you, remembering to maintain an even voice. Once you've tried one sound, try a few others, ensuring that you maintain an even voice free of breaks and strain in your melody. By getting rid of the lyrics and using one sound, you make the song you're working on much easier to sing. Doing so will help to relieve the pressure of any strain you may be experiencing with the words. Then try the words again and notice which word (or the first word, if there are a number of them) that causes you to strain.

13. Recognize problematic uncontrolled vowel formations: When you discover problematic notes, stop singing the melody, identify where the note is on a keyboard, and work out the issue using a scale pattern on one of the vowel and sound combinations that are appropriate for your voice-habit. Once you've worked out the problem, return to the melody and see if you can keep the same feeling as when you sang the note correctly on the exercise. You can also:

• Print off the lyrics double spaced and circle the areas or words you notice are problematic. Remember, the root of the problem is often not the high note itself, but a few words before that usually occur within the critical bridge.

- Refer to the vowel chart chart on page 8 and identify which vowel sound belongs to the problem note by looking in the intended vowel column.

- Try to speak the vowel sound instead of singing it. The vowel shape you produce should be almost identical to the shape you sing with. If in doubt, check your formation in the mirror. Is it the same?

- Above the word write the actual and true vowel sound, and, to the side, write at least three or four other words with the same vowel sound to make sure you sing the correct vowel sound when you arrive at it.

14. Narrow problematic vowels: Many singers unconsciously widen their intended vowel shape in an effort to help reach a higher pitch, creating strain. To relieve strain with exercises or words/sounds on high notes, try the following techniques:

- Identify the problematic vowel sound and use the vowel chart below:

- Find the narrower version of the vowel in the narrowed vowel column. For example, if you are narrowing "AH" to "UH", look for a word example for the "UH" vowel sound, such as "bus". Think of a word with the narrowed vowel that is similar to the word in the lyric, and copy it into your lyric sheet. Think and sing the word with the narrowed vowel rather than the actual vowel.

- Although vowel narrowing can correctly adjust the position of your larynx, and so is a hard and fast temporary solution, it doesn't correctly adjust the space in your mouth for higher pitches. Therefore, vowel narrowing on its own can still create vocal problems if left unchecked. For this reason, once you have a grasp of narrowing, you should next learn how to make the finer adjustments for actually tuning vowels asap; the next step.

Simplified Vowel Assistance for Vocal Strain			
Intended Vowel Sound	Example Words	Narrowed Vowel Sound	Example words
AA	bat, nap, gap	EH	bet, net, get
EH	bet, net, get	AY	bait; nail; gate
AY	bait, nail, gate	IH	bit, knit, give
IH	bit, knit, give	EE	beet, neat, geese
EE	beet, neat, geese	Sing through "OO" lips, or with a "dumb" sound. Can be used with any vowels.	
AH	bought, knock, got	UH	bun, nudge, gust
UH	bus, nudge, gust	EU	book, nook, good
EU	book, nook, good	OH	boat, note, goat
OH	boat, note, goat	OO	boot, noon, goose
OO	boot, noon, goose	Sing through "OO" lips, or with a "dumb" sound. Can be used with any vowels.	

15. Fully tune problematic vowels: Use the vowel tuning concepts in the next chapter to apply advanced techniques to get the optimal alignment possible.

2. The Light Singer

Singers with the light voice-habit may have difficulty transitioning from their high voice fully into their low voice on the low notes when singing songs.

Make sure you sing sounds that help you find your low voice before returning to new exercises or the lyric, otherwise your voice will not adjust properly for the lower pitches, and the extra air can be problematic. As you transition from your upper notes into your lower notes, make sure you fully engage your low voice again. Remember, your lower notes should feel almost identical to a healthy, full-sounding speaking voice.

Use the exercises in the following order if you fall into this voice-habit:

1. Use only the amount of air used in speaking: Some singers blast air on higher or lower notes in an attempt to reach the pitch. This creates a weak sound and a buildup of tension as the delicate vocal cords become overwhelmed with air and have no choice but to tense up to try to resist that air. If you do this, use less air by pronouncing your consonant more. If there isn't a consonant on the sound you're working with, put one on! It will provide crucial assistance to your vocal cords.

2. "Speak" your low voice: Learn how to engage your speaking voice in your low voice by simply speaking your pitches rather than singing them.

3. Develop your low voice: Don't be tempted to spend the majority of your practicing singing effortlessly in your high voice in a light manner just because it's easier! Make sure you spend enough time working the low voice (from G3 to G4 on either side of middle C for most women or middle from D above middle C and below for men) so that you begin to feel familiar with it and it grows stable and strong.

4. Exercises to avoid in the beginning: Avoid soft consonants such as "p", "f" and "h" as they may encourage more airflow rather than less. Also avoid "EE" and "OO" vowels as they encourage rather than reduce the high voice resonance. Scale patterns, such as a 1.5 octave scale, that move you above your low voice for longer sequences of notes will also likely disconnect you from the feeling of the low voice, causing the vocal cords to come apart and your voice to go into a breathy tone again, either in your low ranges or throughout.

5. Use compact scale patterns: Use ascending 5 tone, semi-tone, and octave up scale patterns, as they will allow you to more easily maintain the feeling of the low voice from one note to another. Use the examples given below in the low range below your critical bridge.

6. Use low, open vowels: Use vowel sounds like "AA" ("bat") and "AH" ("father") to build a better sense of the low voice. Try to find stronger vocal cord closure with these vowels before moving on to other vowel sounds.

7. Use hard consonants: "GUG" ("gum") and "GEG" ("get") are more great vowel/consonant combinations for you. Using consonants such as "g" and "n" before your vowels provides a good deal of extra compression to help with the closing of your vocal cords.

8. Use exaggerated, pharyngeal sounds: Using the "AA" vowel sound, sing a short scale pattern with a "witch-like" quality (a cackle, or a twang without going into a nasal sound) to help get the vocal cords to close more strongly so you don't go into a breathy tone. You might have to smile slightly as you do the exercise. As you get "AA" to work in your voice with stronger vocal cords, move on to other sounds at the top of the vowel chart on page 5.

9. Order of vowel work: You should progress through work with every vowel sound ideally in the following order, trying to progressively maintain the ease of vowel production from one vowel to the next: AA/AH/UH/EH/IH/AY/EU/OH/EE/OO.

10. Practice transitioning: Once the low voice strengthens, be sure to practice transitioning from your low voice into your head voice using ascending oriented octave patterns from the lower voice.

11. Change voice-habits when necessary: Once light singers discover and strengthen their low voice, they often begin to experience difficulty releasing the grab of the low voice as they ascend back into their head voice. Make sure you learn to be gentle with your low voice in the beginning and always strive to maintain an even voice throughout. If you find that you begin to strain with your low voice after developing, use the exercises from the strainer voice-habit section above.

3. The Flipper

For singers who don't strain but "flip", or experience a break, in the voice when trying the words, this break shows where the change in resonance and muscle is that the voice must learn to adjust through evenly (unless you choose to let it break as an effect - just don't make it a habit!). If the resonance in the voice isn't allowed to shift properly, it will break.

If you are to experience an even, gradual shift in resonance, you must allow yourself to let go of the feeling of resonance that you previously had in your low range and let your voice shift gradually through your critical break, without going into falsetto. When singing songs, try using one sound at a time that helps you find an even voice through your transitional area on the melody before attempting the words in the lyric.

Use the exercises in the following order if you fall into this voice-habit:

1. Focus on your critical bridge: Focus on developing the areas between your low and high voice by maintaining an even sound.

2. Vowel sounds to avoid in the beginning: Avoid extreme narrow ("EE", "OO") or wide ("AH", "AA") vowels or any other sounds that induce airflow, such as "f" or "sh". These may cause the vocal cords to crack or create a suddenly breathy tone.

3. Scale patterns: Use scale patterns that allow you to sweep through the voice over a wider range to smooth out breaks. Octave up scale patterns are also useful. You can find examples of these scales in the other voice-habits above.

4. Consonants: Use harder consonants similar to the light voice-habit to aid the vocal cords in managing airflow and provide added compression. "G" and "n" are great choices.

5. Sounds to use: Use neutral vowel sounds like "NAY" ("neighbor"), "NEU" ("nook"), "GUH" ("gum"), "GIH" ("give"), and "MMM" using a squeaky voice (imagine the character voice sounds of Marge Simpson and her sisters).

6. Use exaggerated sounds: Add an edgy or squeaky sound to your exercises as you practice, to help keep your vocal cords together as you ascend through your critical bridge from the low to the high voice.

7. Transitioning to the low voice from high notes in songs: If you are having difficulty transitioning back into your low voice from your high notes, sing sounds that help you find your low voice on a melody before returning to the words in the lyric. Otherwise your voice will not adjust properly for the lower pitches, and the extra air can be problematic. As you transition from your upper notes into your lower notes, make sure you fully engage your low voice again. Remember, your lower notes should feel almost identical to a healthy, full-sounding speaking voice.

4. The Balanced Voice

Use the exercises in the following order if you feel that you consistently sing in a balanced voice with fully developed low and high voice and relatively smooth transitions between them. They will strengthen the coordination of a balanced voice throughout your full range. Be attentive to your voice as you do these exercises. If you revert to one of the other voice-habits as you do them, make sure you address the issues that are causing you to lose your coordination before you continue:

1. Sustains: Hold notes through the difficult areas of your range with held notes using vibrato (see the chapter on vibrato for details).

2. Use difficult exercises for your voice-habit: Use exercises that are difficult for your voice-habit, that you were advised to avoid early in your development.

3. Use large interval scale patterns: Use scale patterns with intervals of fourths, fifths, sixths, and octaves or more to improve your ability to shift from one register to another quickly easily.

4. Diminuendo: Practice singing from a gentle intensity to a loud intensity then back to a gentle intensity, all while sustaining one note. This is one of the most advanced skills in singing. Learning to do it well will translate into more emotional landscapes in your singing.

Breaking Free of Your Voice Habit

For more advanced singers, once your voice builds in balance and strength enough that you are well acquainted with a full, even transition through your critical bridge on most vowel sounds, it may be helpful to stop thinking of the voice as divided at all, but as one smooth, continuous, strong voice. Just be careful not to fall back into your old voice-habit.

Find a Teacher

As always, all vocal issues are best diagnosed and handled by an instructor who is trained and experienced in guiding singers through the various registrations of the body without strain. If at all possible, find a teacher in your area trained in assessing voices who can help give some perspective. See the chapter on finding a teacher for more details.

EXERCISES

1) Exercises that work well for my voice are:

_____

_____

2) Exercises I should avoid for now are:

_____

_____

3) Singers I could listen to that would reinforce the good habits I need to build are:

_____

_____

4) Singers I listen to that might reinforce my bad habits are:

_____

_____

5) Using a sound that is easier for you to vocalize, sing the whole melody with it across the whole song. Can you keep an even, balanced voice?

_____

_____

6) Do the same thing with a sound that is more challenging for you. Refer to the suggestions earlier in the chapter if you struggle.

_____

_____

7) Note where the difficult passages of the song are. Can you isolate where the very first sign of tension occurs? How can you address it?

_____

_____

5. THE SWEET SPOT

Goals: Understand how to find the optimal vowel tunings for advanced vocal applications.

Why? It's very invigorating and nourishing to have moments of singing with your full vocal power, and your instinct may demand it. An understanding of vowel tuning will allow you to master the "sweet spot" where your voice feels easy and vibrant, giving you more strength, control, flexibility and enjoyment in your singing.

. . . .

When we look at building our vocal coordination even further, we need to ultimately establish the optimal vocal balance to maximize the amplitude and dynamic flexibility of your voice in a healthy way. This chapter deals with how to achieve that optimal balance through vowel tuning.

But before we do that, we will need to explore in more detail some common misconceptions about what creates a powerful vocal sound. Mastering the sweet spot in your voice requires a good understanding of what produces a strong sound, especially since there are many misconceptions about it, as well as of what tools are available for you to find this optimal coordination.

Strain from Incorrect Belting

Many singers attempt to incorrectly create a powerful "belt" sound by trying to maintain the functionality of the low voice on high notes, that is, without modifying the tuning of their vowels to engage the correct muscle balance or amplifier adjustment for the higher pitch. This creates flat or sharp notes, vocal strain and harsh sounds.

Dynamics

Many singers try to copy the loudness of the singers they love. However, you want to develop your own natural strengths and learn how to express your own instincts, rather than always imposing someone else's on yourself. When you get comfortable with your own sound and have developed enough balance and strength, then you can experiment with the loud dynamics of other singers.

Always resist pushing or getting louder until you can create better coordination and optimal resonance alignments in your voice.

The Secret of Vocal Power

Vocal power is widely misunderstood in the world of singing. Vocal power on high notes comes not from great physical abdominal effort (although feelings of support may be experienced), but from an optimal tuning of vowels for maximum resonant effect that creates a feeling of ease and power simultaneously. This requires aligning with the "sweet spot". By tuning your vowels in this way, you project significantly higher frequencies and overtone patterns more easily, which the listener perceives as a strong vocal sound. The singer may apply little effort relative to the sound produced. Maintaining this alignment in a relaxed fashion, without straining for high notes, is one of the most highly regarded and sought-after singing skills for vocalists.

The listeners' perception of the powerful resonant sounds is that the singer is applying a tremendous amount of effort. Only the singer knows the secret!

Easy Go Lucky

It is much easier to produce lighter, gentler tones than loud ones. Because the resonances of your amplifier provide most of the power in a strong sound, vowel tuning does not have to be optimal.

As we explored in earlier chapters, the vocal cords are extraordinarily tiny, and without amplification wouldn't be capable of producing much sound at all. In a balanced voice, powerful vocal high notes come not as much from the vocal cords themselves but from the harmonics that are amplified above the larynx, where the vocal cords create the basic pitch. When these harmonics align with the formant resonances of a vowel, it creates a massive boost of amplification of the sound. As you achieve the right alignment with your vowels, the energy from the harmonics created through the resonant cavities create a cushioning effect downward upon the vocal cords (aka back-pressure), which provides them with even greater stability so they can vibrate more fully, creating an even stronger boost in amplification. This powerful and exciting process is called acoustic feedback. The more tuned these vowels become, the more powerful the voice can grow. What the listener ends up hearing isn't so much the basic pitch, but the amplified harmonics of that pitch by the resonant spaces of your throat and mouth. However, they perceive the overall sound as belonging to the pitch itself.

Harmonics

Because finding the sweet spot involves accurately adjusting the amplifying spaces of your throat and mouth to align with optimal harmonics of the sung pitch, it is helpful (but not completely necessary) to understand what harmonics are and how they work. If you find this section on harmonics too complex, feel free to skip over to the vowel tuning guidelines just after. The concepts of harmonics can seem quite abstract at first, but can be fascinating as you begin to understand them.

When you sing a basic pitch, the sound waves consist of both the pitch you sang and the series of harmonics that are multiples of that pitch. (The basic pitch is also known as fundamental pitch, harmonic one, or the first harmonic.) If you sing a G below middle C (G3 on a keyboard), its frequency is 196 Hz, or 196 cycles per second. Put simply, your vocal cords are vibrating at 196 times per second!

Each harmonic is a multiple of the pitch. The first harmonic (H1) is the sung pitch itself - in this case 196 Hz. The second harmonic is the pitch doubled, or multiplied by two. The third harmonic is triple the basic pitch, or the basic pitch multiplied by 3. And so on.

The harmonic series of G3 is:

- H1 - G3 - 196 Hz
- H2 - G4 - 392 Hz (one octave higher than basic pitch)
- H3 - D5 - 588 Hz (one octave + major fifth higher than basic pitch)
- H4 F#5 - 784 Hz (one octave + major fifth + major third higher than basic pitch)

This means that singing a G3 note may not pose any significant challenge because the higher overtones aren't particularly high. But suppose you must sing a tenor high C - an octave and a half higher than G3. Here's the harmonic series for C5:

- H1 - C5 - 523.3 Hz
- H2 - C6 - 1046.5 Hz (one octave higher than basic pitch)
- H3 - G6 - 1568 Hz (one octave + major fifth higher than basic pitch)
- H4 - B6 - 1975.5 Hz (one octave + major fifth + major third higher than basic pitch)

The second note, C5, is only an octave and a half higher than G3, the first note. The difference between the basic pitches is just over 200 Hz. But the difference between the harmonics of the two notes is much more vast. The fourth harmonic of C5 is roughly 1200 Hz higher than the fourth harmonic of G3 - six times the difference of the basic pitch. This makes the higher harmonics of C5 much more difficult to "tune" to than G3.

Vowel tuning becomes increasingly necessary the higher the pitch because as the sung pitch gets higher, the harmonics of the pitch multiply, becoming further and further apart, making it increasingly challenging to modify the spaces of your throat and mouth to align with those higher and higher harmonics. The space in your throat is the most problematic because it is a much bigger space than the mouth, and, because a bigger space accentuates lower tones, it is much more limited in its ability to align with higher overtones. So once a harmonic is out of the range of the throat (the space in the throat can no longer get any smaller - the larynx cannot get any higher), it must drop to a lower harmonic to maintain an easy vocal production.

> "The overtones get further apart the higher you sing, so you have to be precise with the vowel to keep it lined up."
>
> - JOHN HENNY

Vowel Tuning Controls

Vowel tuning is essential to finding the sweet spot on every pitch and to maximizing vocal power, both one vowel sound at a time in your vocal exercises and when singing lyrics on specific words, especially on higher notes. In higher ranges, every pitch will require a new adjustment for each vowel to find the optimal setting for that particular pitch and vowel.

The following guidelines assume that you have established some basic balance between your low and high voice through your critical bridge on at least a few basic sounds for your voice-habit. Use these guidelines for improving and maximizing alignment of the sweet spot on those sounds. However, make sure you apply the solutions in earlier chapters for more difficult vowel sounds for your voice-habit before working on the guidelines below for the more challenging vowels. This is because the solutions you require are not only related to the way you shape your vowels (As in the ABCs from chapter one), but may also be related to issues of breath and closure of vocal cords (Bs and Cs). The guidelines below are for adjusting the shapes of vowels made by your amplifier in an already fairly well-coordinated voice.

The vast majority of vowel tuning problems arise from trying to sing high notes while the larynx is at a position too high in the throat. So the first three steps are designed to help establish a slightly deeper, lower larynx on higher pitches. But you must be careful here too. If the larynx is lowered too much, it may still not align with the optimal harmonic, lacking the appropriate amount of energy for a higher pitch. The tone will sound too imposed, dark, or hollow.

Use the rules below as a guide in the following order for problematic high notes that require vowel tuning for finding the sweet spot:

1. Adjust throat space: Note the position of your larynx, using your fingertip to follow your voice-box on the difficult note. Is it rising substantially or uncomfortably high?

- **Use the vowel chart** earlier in the book to either widen or narrow the vowel slightly, which most significantly adjusts the space in the throat, but also the mouth space along with it.

- **Exaggeratedly deepen the larynx.** If the larynx is still too high, try temporarily adding a "dumb" quality (sounds like Yogi the bear) to the sound - what we call a slightly imposed larynx - being careful not to add any extra air as you do it. The higher you are in your range, the more you may feel the inclination of the larynx to rise too much. This means you may need to exaggerate this technique even further to maintain a deeper position for the larynx.

- **Use less exaggeration.** Once you can maintain a low larynx, use less exaggeration while being sure not to let the larynx rise too much - the position should be one where you feel some sense of ease in your note without muscular effort. Check in a mirror, or feel your voice-box with your finger to monitor its movement and ensure it's not too high or too low.

2. Adjust mouth space

- **Adjust the lips,** usually slightly forward towards "OO" on wider vowels (AH/AA/UH/EH, etc) in higher ranges. Too much closing of the lips and your tone will sound too hollow or dumb, and/or create a squeeze or tightness in your throat from the misalignment of harmonics. However, many vowel tuning problems stem from an over-narrowed vowel. In these cases, you may need to do the reverse - incrementally widen the lips slightly. Be careful not to widen too far as that can easily raise the larynx, and throw off its optimal alignment.

- **Incrementally lower the jaw** the more you ascend into your higher registers. Not even jaw drop will create a squeeze in your vowel production. Too much and the words become overly distorted. Make sure as you drop the jaw that you don't open your mouth wide towards a smile.

- **Moving the tongue slightly forward** can create a better alignment by creating a smaller space in your mouth to align with a higher harmonic. Just remember to make sure your larynx doesn't rise with any dramatic changes in the tongue position. Too much movement in the tongue can have the opposite effect of pulling up the larynx and/or creating overly produced words.

Caution

Be careful you don't blow too much air, or create inappropriate tension through tightening any muscles in your throat. Doing so means you've increased the breath pressure from your abdomen too far. Reduce the airflow and find a more spoken sound again before trying again to achieve a stronger sound.

Vowel tuning is precarious work - especially in areas of the voice which you find difficult, and especially without a good teacher trained in vowel tuning. It's very easy to confuse a powerful sound with yelling or excessive use of the low voice, which may cause the pitch to go flat or worse: create vocal damage

that can end your singing enjoyment entirely. Learning to consistently sing in sweet spots can take considerable amounts of careful training by a skilled instructor, especially on higher pitches and through your critical bridge, where optimal vowel production is more challenging.

Again, seeking help from a professional instructor with a well developed ear is essential. It is far too easy to send excessive breath pressure to the tiny vocal cords, endangering them to vocal swelling or vocal nodules.

EXERCISES

1) Using a sound that is easier for you in a challenging area of your voice, see if you can keep the same or similar resonant sensation on the same pitch on other vowels that you find more difficult. What do you need to adjust to maintain your alignment in the sweet spot?

_____

_____

6. VIBRATO

Goals: Allow a natural vibrato to occur wherever there is a sustained (held) note in your singing.

Why? Your voice needs to remain flexible, free, and as dynamic as possible. Many of the notes you sing will be sustained. In general, there should always be vibrato when you dwell on a note, otherwise the vocal cords may over-tighten and you will sound off-pitch. Vibrato is essential to a balanced voice, and is expected in nearly every musical genre.

. . . .

The term "vibrato" is borrowed directly from Italian, and means "to vibrate". When you hear a singer produce vibrato correctly, the pitch they are sustaining is highlighted by an oscillation of about a semi-tone above and below the actual sustained pitch. This oscillation is very quick - a cycle of about 7 times a second in a healthy vibrato! The oscillation of pitch is subtle, however - you should predominantly hear the pitch you are sustaining, not the pitches above or below.

Slow   Fast

Vibrato Speed

In a well balanced voice, vibrato occurs naturally on any sustained pitch. In the beginning of training, you may find that you can only get a straight tone in your singing, or that vibrato doesn't occur when and where you intend it to. Have no fear. Over time, using the exercises below will help you become more familiar with the sensation of vibrato, so you will be able to control it at will.

How to Practice

As you practice the exercises below, even though the note you are singing will oscillate above and below the pitch, the core of your tone should always be the note you are singing, not the oscillations. Be careful you don't get caught in oscillating too much to the note above or below so that the root note itself becomes blurry - flat (slightly below) or sharp (slightly above) of the pitch you are intending to sing. Be attentive to the healthy vibrato of other singers, and try to emulate their vibrato with your own voice.

When I teach vibrato to students who do not have a strong experience of it, I use the following 5-step process:

1. Start with an outward pant. Take a breath in, and on your outward breath, pant while vocalizing using an "OO" sound ("boot") with staccato. If you do it right, you should sound like a gorilla!

2. Keep the pant-like oscillation of airflow, but move from staccato to continuous airflow so it's not broken as in the exercise above, but keep the pant feeling from the tummy. As you do this, don't let the sound go straight (no vibrato), become stuttered, or get uneven. Try to maintain a consistent, loose pulse of air from the pant with a steady, unbroken stream.

3. Allow the pulse of air to slightly bump the pitch above the one you are singing as you maintain the loose pulse of air from the exercise above, loosely. It should bounce up and back down repeatedly, each bump created by a pulse of air. You want to maintain a steady, unbroken stream of air with a pulsing bounce. Try this oscillation at a slow speed of about one to two times a second.

4. Allow the oscillation to speed up, very gradually, as you become comfortable with the oscillation that is triggered by the pulse of air. Do not attempt to speed up too soon or too fast, or you will lose the oscillation and the coordination. This process can take some singers some time - anywhere from a week to a few months to get right. Have patience, and remain focussed on a natural vibrato.

5. Sing four beats clearly separated (staccato) followed by four counts of beats that are tied together without breaks, still oscillating slightly in pitch, as in the steps above, to the rhythm of a metronome (several are available free online) set to 140 bpm. Be sure your sung pitch highlights the pitch you are trying to add vibrato to - make sure it doesn't accent too much the lower or upper pitch. Go back and forth between the four staccato notes and the four tied oscillating notes. Breaking the notes up with staccato helps to maintain a bounce in the vibrato and stops it from going straight-tone.

Note that the pant should be gentle and subtle - it is not forceful or tense from the stomach. Make sure each pitch oscillation occurs from the slight push of breath from the pant, not by deliberately singing the pitches up and down. The effect should be bounce-like, exaggeratedly slow and slightly breathy. Over time, the oscillation should increase to five to seven times a second until it blossoms into a natural, easy, free sound that occurs on its own whenever a pitch is held. As with most exercises, practice your vibrato with an easy dynamic - that is, not too loud or too quiet. Start lightly, and increase your vocal cord closure, or intensity, as your coordination improves. Above all, have patience. Developing a natural-sounding vibrato can take some time.

Vibrato Speed

Maintain an even but slow, exaggerated speed in the beginning, allowing the vibrato to speed up in its own time - don't try to force a faster speed too soon or the vibrato will go stiff again. If you can, resist letting the tone lose its bounce, with no oscillation at all. Let each pant bump the pitch up and into oscillation.

THE MUSICAL IMPULSE

"Rhythm is probably the most important thing for any musician to master. You can hit wrong notes and get by but if the rhythm is wrong, everyone is gonna know it right away. You have to keep up with where the pulse is and connect with it."

- JAMAL MOHAMED

7. LISTENING

Goals: Be aware of all the major changing elements within the music – the instruments, other sound relationships, solos, volume changes, and crescendos, however minor, and envision the changing movement of the melody across the whole song.

Why? Listening to and perceiving the various elements that make up a song allows you to plan and navigate your songs easily, stay in tune, and get the most out of your creativity.

. . . .

I began working with "Luanne" after she had come to me looking to explore songs by a famous songwriter that she had grown fond of. Although she didn't experience any major issues with her range, she had grown somewhat disenchanted with her inability to keep her singing interesting, modern, and fresh. Her singing always seemed steady at one dynamic, her vibrato was constant on all her held notes, and she felt at a distance emotionally to what she was singing about.

We began by breaking down the structure of her song. Where were the choruses and verses? What was the story that was unfolding in each part? How did the mood and energy change in each section? Once Luanne began to look at her song and discern the parts

> "Two things control men's nature, instinct and experience."
>
> - BLAISE PASCAL

like a painting (Luanne was also an abstract painter), she started to find nuances in her singing that matched her understanding of the song. She began to hear the different instruments play their role. She could feel how and in what ways each instrument seemed to spur on the melody she was singing. She slowly began to become more playful against the various elements of her song, and it wasn't long before she broke out of her constant vibrato, too! She was soon more instinctual with her singing, more trustworthy of her impulses to do different things, and began to find new ways of expressing the lyrics and melody.

This was a profound experience for Luanne. After singing through a song we had been working on, she sat back against her stool in amazement at what she had just done. "I've never sung like that before. It was electrifying," she said. "It was like the lyrics and my singing were just moving through me, and I didn't have to think about it at all." She has since found more satisfaction from her singing than ever before.

Studying the Greats

There are plenty of singers you can learn from in every genre who can/ could sing easily through their critical bridge across all their registers, with musicality and instinct: Ella Fitzgerald, Sarah Vaughan, Tony Bennett (jazz), Michael Jackson, Barbra Streisand, Lady Gaga, Kate Bush (pop), Paul McCartney, Adam Lambert, Jeff Buckley (rock), Joni Mitchell (folk), Wendy Moten, Stevie Wonder, Luther Vandross, Aretha Franklin, Eva Cassidy (soul), Luciano Pavarotti, Robert Weede (opera), Julie Andrews, Maureen McGovern, Dawn Upshaw, Kristin Chenoweth, and Anthony Warlow (musical theatre). These singers all sang with a vocal freedom and intensity that was striking, rich, and powerful – yet somehow seemed bafflingly easy.

What this means is that if you want to learn to sound as great as the singers you admire, to borrow from their tricks, to learn their subtleties, you have to immerse yourself in their work.

Listening is an important skill for any vocalist. Learning how to become more aware of the music and other voices allows you to hone your own skills and musicianship further and faster.

Join a Choir

Some of the most successful vocalists of our time started singing in choir. Whiney Houston, Aretha Franklin, Bobby McFerrin, Tina Turner, and many more all got their crucial start in their church choir. You don't necessarily have to participate in a church choir either. There are many community choirs as well as smaller group ensembles that can help get you started.

A choir setting provides fertile ground for the development of essential listening skills. It will train your musical ear and your voice to precisely match pitch and teach you the basics of contemporary musical structure by solidifying your understanding of rhythmic and structural ideas. It also teaches you to align with the objectives of a group.

Listening for Song Structure

In order for your singing instinct to improve, you must also add the actual experience of singing. Through frequent, repeated experiences, your instinct will become more natural. But it can take time to learn to discern the various subtler elements in a song. With the slick production of songs these days, it is sometimes very challenging!

Here are the 6 main elements you should listen for as a singer when analyzing a song:

- Song structure
- Instrumentation
- Story
- Voice
- Movement of energy and mood
- Movement and contour of melody

Broad Song Structure

How your song is structured will play the strongest role in dictating what is most appropriate for you to do vocally. As a vocalist, you need to always understand and listen to where you are in the song so you can increase or decrease energy as required to suit your interpretation. It also paves the way for a better understanding of music as a vocalist, and teaches you to structure your own musical ideas in the future, giving you plenty of opportunities to experiment.

Song Structure and Letter Names

Musical Phrases: If you put a melody two or more bars of music (a group of musical beats of equal duration forming a rhythmic segment that repeats) together you begin to form musical phrases. These phrases added together extend into verses, and verses into choruses, and then into full length songs. Typically, you may express a thought or part of a sentence in about two bars of music.

The Verse: Usually, those 2 bars will repeat in a similar but slightly different fashion about four times to form a more complete thought, a bit like a paragraph. Varying the same melody slightly four times to create 8 bars, or 8 measures of music, forms the melodic backbone to almost every song in western music. 8 bars form a block of time, usually a complete verse, that can be repeated throughout the song with different words, different rhythms, different tonality, etc - but the gist remains the same. A verse is essentially a series of thoughts that form a paragraph or two. It creates the environment and the mood of the song. In terms of song structure, verses are often called the "A section".

Pre-Chorus: While having one section of music that repeats can help make the song memorable, having just one musical "idea" like this can get boring. We love to hear variety. What songwriters and composers often do is come up with an interesting contrast. We could call this contrasting section the "lift section": it lifts the song into the chorus. The lift section helps intensify the energy of the song beyond the energy in the verse, as it leads up to the chorus.

The Chorus: The chorus is usually the part of the song which has the hook - the part that is most memorable and that drives the energy of the song, "hooking" us into the song and leaving us singing it well after the song ends. It's usually the most energetic point of the song, so that whenever the song returns to the chorus it creates a kind of excitement. The verses really serve to create a buildup to the chorus. There may be any number of verses before a chorus, and there may be any number of choruses. It all depends on the characteristics and energy of the song, and the temperament of the songwriter. We could call the chorus the "B section" (although it is also often called "C").

The Bridge: In most songs, there is a third section that gives more variety. We could call this the "C section" - most often referred to as the "bridge". The bridge is a section of a song, usually occurring only once towards the end that breaks the familiarity of the repeating sections adding something new; a kind of spice to the music. The bridge adds flavor, usually before returning one last time to a verse or chorus. You might show the sections in a song with a bridge in it as: ABABCAB.

Putting Them Together

Most songs have a verse, chorus, and a bridge section. There may also be an instrumental section (the guitar solo in section 8 in the example below riffs on the verse structure, or the "A section"), an intro, and/or an outro. The example below lays out the structure of No Doubt's song "Don't Speak". A is the verse, B is the pre-chorus, C is the chorus, and

D is the bridge. You can put any letter name to any part of the song as long as it makes sense to you and the musicians following you.

Song example: Don't Speak (No Doubt):

- Section 1: A - Verse 1
- Section 2: B - Pre-chorus
- Section 3: C - Chorus
- Section 4: A - Verse 2
- Section 5: B - Pre-chorus
- Section 6: C - Chorus
- Section 7: D - Bridge
- Section 8: A - Instrumental
- Section 9: C - Chorus
- Section 10: C - Chorus
- Section 11: C - Outro and fade

Instrumentation

Once you understand the broad structure of a song, you should be able to discern the various instruments that create each of them. When you're listening to songs, see if you can pick out the various instruments such as the drums (kick, snare, high hats, cymbals, rim-shots, toms), lead guitar, rhythm guitar, bass, piano/keyboards, percussion (tambourine, bongos etc). Note which instruments appear in the verses and choruses and if certain repeats of the verses or chorus have added or removed instruments, and how that affects and enhances the mood. The instrumentation for the sections of "Don't Speak" are given below:

Song example: Don't Speak (No Doubt):

- Section 1: A - Verse 1 (lead vocals & guitar only)
- Section 2: B - Pre-chorus (background vocals & guitar only)
- Section 3: C - Chorus (drums, bass, guitar, strings, lead/BG vocals)
- Section 4: A - Verse 2 (guitar, strings, lead vocals)
- Section 5: B - Pre-chorus (lead/BG vocals, drums, guitar, bass, guitar)
- Section 6: C - Chorus (drums, bass, guitar, strings, lead/BG vocals)

- Section 7: D - Bridge (drums, bass, guitar, strings, lead/BG vocals)
- Section 8: A - Instrumental (Guitar solo)
- Section 9: C - Chorus (drums, bass, guitar, strings, lead/BG vocals)
- Section 10: C - Chorus (drums, bass, guitar, strings, lead/BG vocals)
  Section 11: C - Outro and fade

The Story

Every song tells a story. Ask yourself what is motivating the words in the song: Who, what, where, when, how, and why? Become the storyteller. Establish who you are in the song, who is in the story, and who you are singing to. There is no limitation here – be creative! The more wild and adventurous your choices are, the more wild you can give your singing permission to be.

Ask yourself: What's the story this song is telling? Where are you when you're telling the story? When is the story happening? How is the story being told (first, second, or third person)? Most importantly, WHY are you telling the story??? Why would your listener be interested? What is the context of the story? When are you telling the story - are you engaged in the story as it is happening, or are you recalling the story from memory? Or is it a combination of both?

As with any story, in a song there should be a setup, development of the story, climax, and then resolution. Understanding these elements can help you deepen your ability to communicate the story you are telling when you sing a song. How does the story unfold in each verse and chorus? How does the lyric create and affect the energy in the music?

Energy, Movement & Mood

Michael Jackson's "The Way You Make Me Feel" has a consistent energy throughout. But what about Whitney Houston's rendition of "I Will Always Love You"? Its energy is very different. The song's hook occurs in the first line of the chorus, but each time you hear it, it builds very slowly to a final climactic ending.

The great psychologist Carl Jung understood the power of energy. He claims that when you understand this energy, you can draw great power from it. All songs have peaks and valleys in their energy. This allows for subtle builds and releases which provide an enormous amount of power for vocalists. Where are the peaks and valleys of your story? When is there a build-up of energy in the story?

> "The greater the tension, the greater is the potential. Great energy springs from a correspondingly great tension of opposites."
>
> - C. G. JUNG

A song generates its energy and magnetism through playing with tension and mood, mainly via consonance and dissonance (see the section on intervals below). A song might start off with a flirtatious light movement of energy that hints at something stronger, or it might drop into the song full speed ahead. It may start quietly with little energy and build slowly towards a climactic all the way through the song. It might build and swell in a particular spot and retreat back towards the end. It's important to notice how the song's energetic movement and its overall energetic feeling evolve over time so you can vary your interpretation and the dynamics of your voice in your singing.

It's helpful to thoroughly understand the movement of the original melody over the length of the song. You should know where the peaks and valleys of the melody are so you can be sure to stay on track as you build momentum, and so that you know how and where to create dramatic surprises, builds, and emotional tension. For instance, you don't want to introduce too much variation on a melody that seems simple in the beginning if you know that later in the song the melody becomes much more interesting and varied. Having this kind of awareness can help you build the right kind of anticipation and emotional swells.

The "Big Moment"

You should take note of where to accentuate moments in the song that should have the most intensity, as that's where your emotions will be most revealing. They will show how you really feel about the song, and whether or not you are genuinely committed to your performance. Many people will pay to see an entire show just for the ecstatic high point of one song. So make sure you know where that moment occurs and that you hit it home!

High notes usually act as a climax to the melody, and should be treated as such. High vocal notes create a sympathetic fast frequency vibration in our bodies and ears and we can't help but get caught up in it! Such is the power of tension in high notes. This is why voice training is so important for singers – high notes can be quite precarious. Understanding where they are and how to align correctly with them helps you prepare the way you approach the entire melody.

The Voice

For each song, consider how the singer - or you - will use his/her/your voice in the context of all the things that are happening in the song. Do they start the first few verses in a breathy tone or even a whisper? Do they get louder in the choruses? How do they communicate emotion? What sound effects do they use? Do they use more licks and embellishments in some areas, but keep it simple in others? How do they add other stylistic elements to their vocal? Are there key moments where embellishments would sound great? All these things can be used as tools for you as a singer in the future.

EXERCISES

1) Break down a song you love into its parts (verse/chorus etc):

    Song and artist: _____

    Section 1:_____

    Section 2:_____

    Section 3:_____

    Section 4:_____

    Section 5:_____

    Section 6:_____

2) Choose a song you love with a simple melody. In the chart on the next page, write the first four sections of the song in the left-hand column. Assuming there are four lines to every section, use a graph line to indicate the contour of the song's melody over time throughout those first four sections. Draw a line that shows roughly how the song's melody moves from the lowest notes to the highest notes over time, and indicate moments where there is the most intensity by drawing the line more thickly.

Do you feel like any other kind of mark would accentuate the song's structure visually? For example, are there one or two important rhythmic nuances that add to the song's feel in that section? If so, draw them in. Add whatever else you feel best represents the melody's development visually.

Song:	Notes	Line 1	Line 2	Line 3	Line 4
Section 1:	Highest ↕ Lowest				
Section 2:	Highest ↕ Lowest				
Section 3:	Highest ↕ Lowest				
Section 4:	Highest ↕ Lowest				

3) In the boxes in the chart below, list the first four structural parts of each song (for example, verse 1, chorus 1, verse 2, bridge). Also fill in: song structure (AABA etc), what instruments are used in each section, how the story evolves in each section, how the singer uses their voice in each section, what the general energetic feeling or mood of the song is for that section, and where the peaks and valleys in the melody's contours are. There is also a third column for you to try your own song.

Song name	Viva La Vida (Coldplay)	Irreplaceable (Beyoncé)	
Structure			
Instruments			
Story			
The voice			
Energy			
Melodic contours			

8. KEEPING TIME

Goal: Tap, clap, or snap to the music as you sing a song on a simple melody. Gradually work towards more complex melodies while keeping time.

Why? Some believe that keeping time is even more important than being precise with the pitches themselves. Knowing how time is divided in music is essential to being able to keep time and sing on time accurately as a singer. If your timing isn't strong, the rhythmic patterns of your melodies will become blurry, like an out-of-focus picture, or even unrecognizable. It won't sound or feel right, and you won't be able to engage your full creative capacity or fully enter into the music.

. . . .

I always learn the most from students who experience a number of issues with their voices. One student in particular - we shall call her Becky - was having a difficult time staying on pitch when she first came to me. The music would start playing and she would stumble through the song's melody at a loss for when to begin singing, how to catch up once she became lost, and when her phrases ended. She seemed to be awash in a sea of musical signals without knowing which she was supposed to follow. The most significant result was that she often sang noticeably out of tune.

The problem with Becky wasn't that she couldn't understand the notes she was supposed to sing - she could hit them when she sang the melody on her own. The problem was that she didn't understand how to take her musical cues from the music for when to start singing. She was endlessly playing catch-up with the music!

Immediately, we began working on her understanding of rhythm.

As Becky began to understand how the music cycled, like the wheels-within-wheels of a clock, she was able to identify how the music's structure unfolded over time. She learned how to pick out where exactly she should start singing her line, how the song unfolded, where the breaks in the melody were, and how to keep up with the music.

The result was magical. In a matter of just a few sessions of rhythmic work, Becky was able to keep time with the music as she sang. Not only that, but 95% of her pitching issues had disappeared. She felt delighted and connected to her singing, and she could be completely present with the message and lyric of her song.

> "An artist must possess Nature. He must identify himself with her rhythm, by efforts that will prepare the mastery which will later enable him to express himself in his own language."
>
> - HENRY MATISSE

When learning to sing in a modern way, it's very important to be able to incorporate rhythmic elements. Rhythm is even important in visual art - as Henry Matisse points out, the artist must align with the pulse of nature. On a very basic level, you should be able to count each beat with a snap, tap of the foot, or a clap, as you sing a song. If you lose the tempo as you sing, you may have a tendency to fall out of sync with the song's rhythm. Have no fear. By focussing on keeping time for a few weeks, your singing will improve dramatically.

Beats Per Minute

Musical time rearranges real time to serve a musical purpose. To understand rhythm, you need to understand how music is broken up over time through the use of notes.

A beat or a note in music is a sound with a particular pitch and duration. You could think of every second on the clock as a beat of music, where each beat has a duration of 1 second. In this way, in one passing minute, you would have passed through 60 beats, each exactly the same duration.

In music you would call that pace, or that tempo of notes, 60 beats per minute: 60 bpm. Now if you slow down this pace of notes by half, so there are half as many notes in a minute, you would only have 30 beats for every minute that passes, or 30 bpm. In this kind of rhythm, you have more space between each beat - two seconds, or twice as much as 60pm. Each beat strikes every other second only.

But even at 60 bpm there is a lot of space between each beat. Unless you figure out a way to keep track of what's supposed to happen in the space in between, you might get lost! In music, you need a way to structure this time to make sense of it.

The Bar

If the second hand chimes 60 times per minute, but the sound of each passing second ticking away is the same as all the others, then none of the beats will be accented or louder than the others. Imagine instead that as each second ticks away, it chimes the first of every four beats a little louder than the others. If this happened, you would hear a kind of cycle with four beats in every cycle. You would call this cycle of four beats one measure, or one bar.

In contemporary music, you almost always hear accented beats and that's part of what gives music its pulsating rhythm.

The Downbeat

We call the note at the beginning of every bar, or the first of every four beats, the "downbeat", because that beat sets down the beginning of a new cycle of beats. Although the downbeat isn't always sounded or played louder and is often just implied, it's how musicians usually get their bearings in the rhythm of a song. Changes in the music's chord structure (the combination of notes played at the same time by the instruments are its chord; the combination of chords in a song determine its chord structure) often occur on the downbeat. For example, in the song "Hey Jude", the word "Jude" always lands on the downbeat, and the song's chord changes frequently occur on the downbeat as well.

Time Signature

A bar with four beats in a measure would be in "4/4" (pronounced "four four") time or "common" time. This means that every bar is counted in terms of four notes, or 4/4. A bar with only three beats in a measure would be in "3/4" time - meaning three beats to every bar, not four. We call 3/4 or 4/4 the "time signature" of a song. Another common time signature is 6/8 (6 eighth notes to every bar of music), but 3/4 and particularly 4/4 are the most widely used in modern music.

Locating the First Beat of Every Bar

The first beat of every bar is crucial in understanding rhythm and being able to follow the music. Often the first beat in every bar of music is slightly accented, but just as often it is not. So it may take some time to identify the first beat in every bar.

> "If you could sing from your heart and keep time, that's it! That's all I know."
>
> - RAY CHARLES

To find the first beat, locate the cycles of beats in the music. If you struggle, go to your local library or search online and find the sheet music for the song. See if you can find the downbeat in the music notation, and learn how to hear it.

Keeping Time

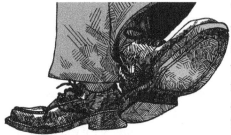 When you're keeping time with music, you can tap, snap, or clap along. To tap, your toes should land on the floor on every beat and come off the floor in between the beats. You may find that in certain points of the song, or in the sheet music you are studying, it is difficult to maintain the rhythm, for example where a rhythmic subtlety in the melody (usually on an off-beat) throws you out of sync. Try to establish at which section of the lyric you lost time, and break down the rhythm to see if you can nail it. Then try again to keep your tapping consistently on time.

EXERCISES

1) Get out a metronome (available online) and set it for 60 bpm. See if you can tap every beat of every measure to that speed. Once you master that, work your way up to 90 bpm without losing time.

2) Starting at 60 bpm again, clap only the first beat of every measure. Then clap only the first and third beat of every measure. Then clap only the second and fourth beat of every measure. See if you can build up to 90, then 120 bpm.

3) For the song "Hey Jude", what is the time signature? Is it 3/4 or 4/4? See if you can pick out where the accented beats are. It may be more noticeable when the entire band comes in later in the song.

_____

_____

4) Listen to Savage Garden's "I Knew I Love You" and write out the lyrics for the first verse and chorus in the boxes below. Each box represents 1 bar - there are 8 boxes in total, 1 for each bar in the first verse. Remember that some phrases may start before the downbeat or before a bar begins. For example, in this song, "I knew I loved..." is sung before the downbeat in the first bar of the chorus, and the first measure begins halfway through "loved".

Verse 1:

Maybe it's intu -	ition
Somethings you just don't ques	tion
	I know

Pre-Chorus:

that it might sound more	than a lit- tle
crazy...	

Chorus:

5) Try the same exercise for a song of your choice and indicate whether each section is chorus/verse etc:

Song Title: _____

Section 1:_____

Section 2:_____

Section 3:_____

6) Play/sing a song that is relatively simple that you enjoy, and clap or snap to the accented beats as the song plays. Can you get through the whole song without losing your time? If not, can you figure out what parts of the melody throw you off the rhythm?

_____

_____

7) Use a metronome to establish the tempo of the song you chose, and then turn the song off. Can you sing the song to the metronome without the music playing and still keep good time?

9. NOTE DURATIONS

Goal: Identify and re-create basic rhythmic patterns with your voice to a set slow tempo, and over time a faster tempo.

Why? If the different pitches of a melody only changed exactly on every beat, it would sound very uninteresting. The melody wouldn't have a conversational or musical feel to it at all. Songwriters vary the rhythms of the melody to reflect the patterns in speech and to keep the song interesting. You need to understand how melodies vary rhythmically so you can be accurate and natural-sounding when you sing the melody.

. . . .

I n order to develop a strong Singer's Instinct, you need to learn how to become playful with rhythm beyond just the basic beats of a bar. To do that, you need to understand how to break down rhythmic notation. In music, we divide time with the following notation notation:

Whole Notes

A whole note is held for the entire bar, covering the space of four quarter notes. It receives a count of four beats. It looks like an O in a classic font. Because a whole note has a value of four quarter notes, only a song in 4/4 time can use whole notes. A song in 3/4 time could only have three quarter notes in a bar, so a whole note couldn't be used (you would instead use a dotted half note - more on that below).

Whole Rests

If the rhythm rests for an entire bar, you won't hear anything for the duration of the bar. It's equal to four quarter beats if in 4/4 time. We call that amount of time a whole rest. In notation, it looks like an upside down hat on the staff line.

Rhythm Value Tree

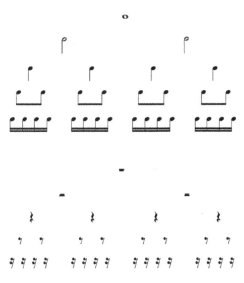

In the image to the left, you can see how the value of a whole note in music breaks down into smaller values. In the image below it are the values for rests, or pauses in music. All of the combined values on every row are equal to one whole note as in the top image, or one whole rest as in the bottom. In the image above, all of the notes (except the whole note) have stems that are "upside down" pointing downward. The notes can also have stems that are right side up, point upward, as in the examples outlined below.

Quarter-Notes

In North American music we refer to beats as "quarter notes", because every note gets a beat of a duration of one quarter of the value of the whole bar. A bar in 4/4 time for instance will have four quarter notes to every bar, while a bar of music in 3/4 will have three quarter notes to a bar. A quarter note looks like a filled-in black circle with a stem. In the notation below, each quarter notes gets a count.

Half Notes

 If a quarter note is held over the space of two quarter notes, the note then becomes the value of two quarter notes put together - a half note. It's held for two quarter beats. It looks like an empty dot with a stem:

Now we will examine these notes put together to form rhythm sequences in notation. Below is a musical staff, made up of five horizontal lines, also known as "staff lines", which represent both pitch (how high or low each note is) and rhythm (how quickly or slowly each note is held). Notes that show exclusively rhythm aren't usually pitch specific, but in the rhythmic examples below the notes are all written on the middle staff line.

Above the notation are the counts (shown in numbers) indicating the count values that are included in each note. You could count these out loud or in your head as you tap or clap the rhythmic values in each bar. For example, the first half note would receive the count one and two, while the second half notes gets the count three and four. Tap/clap only on the first beat as you count out loud all four beats in the bar in time:

Eighth Notes

 When two beats of equal duration are in the space of one quarter note, we call them eighth beats - two eighth beats are equal to one quarter note. In music notation an eighth note looks like a quarter note, but has a tail added to its stem. If there are two eighth notes together in the same beat, their tails are connected together. In the notation below, you would pronounce "and" where the + is. For example, out loud (or silently) you would count "one and two and three and four and (repeat) one and two and ...":

Sixteenth Notes

 When two beats of equal duration occur in the space of one eighth note, we call them sixteenth notes - 2 sixteenth beats are equal to one eighth note. In music notation, a sixteenth note looks like an eighth note, but has two tails added to its stem, instead of one. If there are two sixteenth notes together in the same eighth beat, their tails are connected together:

In the notation below, because the beats are sixteenth notes, you would count the spaces between each of the eighth notes as: "one ee and ah two ee and ah three ee and ah...":

Quarter Rests

 Sometimes a rhythm may skip a beat where no sound is made. To mark this "rest", there is a gap where a quarter note should be - a quarter rest. In music notation, it looks similar to a squiggly closing bracket:

Half Rests

 Sometimes a rhythm can skip two beats, or two quarter notes. When this happens, we call that a half rest. In music notation it looks like a hat, right side up.

Dotted Notes

If there is a dot after a note, it indicates that the note value is the original value plus one half of the value of the note. If it's a dotted quarter note, as in the example to the right, it means the time value of that note is one quarter plus one eighth, or one and a half beats in the bar.

Other Common Notation Symbols

In the image to the left, the symbol on the far left side is a treble clef, notating how you would reference the letter note values relating to note frequency (we will not examine letter note values in this book, although you are encouraged to learn more on your own). The "C" tells you that the the piece is in "common time", or 4/4. Therefore, each bar has a value of four quarter notes. Both bars in the example have whole rests in each bar and the entire example is only two bars long. The last bar is marked with a double line which marks it as the last bar, or the end bar of a song.

Repeat Bar Lines

When there are two bar lines, with one noticeably thicker accompanied by two dots in the middle spaces of the staff line, it indicates that you should repeat the bars between them once (or as otherwise indicated) before continuing. In the examples above and below, there are repeat bar lines inside every bar. This means you would play each bar twice (or more if you like for practice) before moving on to the next. This should help you get a better feel for the rhythm as you go from one rhythm sequence in one bar to the next.

In the first bar below, the last beat is two eighth notes - receiving two claps in one beat. As you keep time, these notes would be on counts: "three and" over the two eighth notes. In the second bar, the first beat is a dotted quarter. It receives counts "one and two" while the note eighth note after falls on the "off" beat. This can take a bit of practice to get right.

As you count out loud the numbers above the bar ("one and two and..."), tap or clap the following rhythms:

EXERCISES

Using the rhythms below do the exercises that follow:

1) Taking one bar at a time, see if you can tap, snap, clap or sing (on a sound that is comfortable for you) the following rhythms to a speed of 30 bmp (use a metronome), as you count out the time ("1 and 2 and...") out loud, or silently. Gradually speed up to 60 bpm, then 120 bpm.

2) Under the beats write "dap" for quarter notes, "doo" for eighth notes on the beat, and "ba" for eighth notes on off beats (the second eighth note). Speak those sounds as you keep count.

3) Do the previous exercise, but try singing the notes on different pitches in a comfortable range, whatever comes to mind, as you sing the rhythmic counts. Do any melodies come to mind?

4) Find the sheet music to a song you love. See if you can tap/clap the rhythms in the main melody.

10. RHYTHM'S MORSE CODE

Goals: Stay "in the groove" of a song when you sing, and be able to identify and/or add your own syncopation elements to the melody.

Why? The band and/or the music itself creates and informs the groove or rhythmic feel of the song, often through syncopation or swing. It's essential to know how each instrument plays in relationship to the pulsing beat, directly influencing how you sing your melodies. Otherwise, you may not sound musical in relation to the music.

. . . .

T he concept of "groove" is difficult to define, yet is essential to being able to feel the song and effectively communicate with other musicians. Groove is the result of all the rhythmic elements created by the music that beg the listener to tap along. As a singer, you should feel the groove of a song just as much as the other musicians who are playing it. Genres that typically have a strong sense of groove are rock, soul, funk, R&B, and gospel - they typically  inspire us to dance or shout out. But even genres that call for a more laid-back feel still have a swinging groove within them, a rhythmic sense, albeit more subtle.

Listening

The groove of a song is created by the rhythm section (drums, bass, guitar and keyboards). It's important for you to hone your awareness of the groove section of all the songs you sing so you can live in the groove and play off it more strongly and creatively. The rhythmic sense of the groove creates an important backdrop for the context in which the message or meaning of the song will be delivered by you. Even minor changes to the rhythm can dramatically alter the sense of the groove, and thus the entire feel of the song. Be sensitive to how the groove of your songs changes over time: From first verse to chorus; from chorus to second verse, etc (more on song structure in the next section).

Beat Accents

Most contemporary popular songs, particularly in R&B, soul, jazz, and gospel, heavily accent the second and fourth beats in their rhythms. Other genres such as rock or musical theatre may accent more strongly the first and third beats of the song. In opera, beats in a bar, and even the bars themselves, may barely be accented at all!

In music, these accents are louder than the other instruments, and can easily overpower the other sounds - including your singing. Becoming aware of the accents will greatly influence how you should sing, suggesting whether you should sing with, on either side of, or against the accents of the song through syncopation, depending on the demands of the melody, instrumentation, song, and your Singer's Instinct. For instance, you may choose to disregard accenting the beats in your singing altogether, keeping a flowing feeling, or you may accent only notes that occur right after the beats to create a sophisticated rhythmic effect. In all cases, understanding where the accents land in the beats of the song is one of the most important factors to singing in the "pocket" (a feeling of singing or playing exactly in sync with all the elements in the music).

Most accented rhythms in modern music fall on the second and fourth beats of every bar (notice not on the first beat). Being able to anchor your singing around these accented beats will develop your musical listening skills and help you to stay aligned with the music similarly to the other musicians, allowing you to sing more effectively and creatively with them, especially at faster tempos where counting every beat just isn't feasible. It will also imbue your singing with magic, and help transport you more deeply into the music's unique landscape.

Groove

Groove is often based on accented rhythms in the music. When listening to music, you want to become aware of rhythmic accents and nuances from other instruments. What are the rhythms that each instrument is playing? How do the rhythm and notes from one instrument affect those of another playing at the same time? How do all the instruments playing together create an overall groove, or feel?

Swing

A good swing isn't just a technique for the golf course! Most styles, including jazz, blues, gospel, R&B, rock, and others "swing" the rhythm by dividing each quarter beat into two, that is into eighth notes. Rather than playing both eighth beats with the same length each, the first eighth note is held a little longer than the second, which is a little shorter. The beat is divided into three, or a triplet rather than two, but you only play the first and third beat, while the first and second note are tied together being twice the value of the last. Singing eighth notes as if the first eighth was longer than the second one, rather than a straight eighth time, adds a bounce effect, a swing, to the melody!

Swing "Slow" Sweet Chariot

How much you swing the beat, that is, how much you delay the second part of the beat, is completely up to the musicians, or you and your tastes. With slower tempos, swing sounds better more exaggerated with the first beat much longer than the second, and faster tempos sound better a little more straight eighths, with the swing not quite as exaggerated.

Syncopation

In music, very few styles put all the rhythmic accents strictly on the main beats. If it did that, the music would sound like a march. This is great for some styles of music, but a lot of modern music uses syncopation, placing the accents elsewhere. Syncopation helps make the song more interesting and sophisticated by playing with the expectation of the accents in the rhythm. It plays on surprise, by accenting some of the weaker beats in the measure irregularly - notes that aren't on the main beats of the song. When done right, these kinds of accents create a kind of rhythmic surprise that adds variety and fun to your singing.

In modern music, syncopation is very important. It provides a sense of musical elegance and a refined style. Syncopation allows you to accent the offbeats in the melody, the ends of your phrases, a point just before the end of your phrase, a word in the middle of your phrase, or somewhere completely at random! All of these tricks add creativity and dynamics that can heighten and intensify your instincts as a singer.

Because of Michael Jackson's background growing up watching and listening to James Brown, his music inherited very strong rhythmic sensibilities. In his song "The Way You Make Me Feel", he places syncopation all throughout his melody, as he often does in most of his music. Notice when he sings the actual line "the way you make me feel" the way he emphasizes the end word "feel" (sometimes he makes the note louder, sometimes he alters the pitch) which he sings between the fourth beat and the first beat of the next bar. Because he anticipates the first beat by placing emphasis on the word just before it, he provides a forward-propelling momentum to the melody, almost like a train moving steadily forward. Notice that he frequently places emphasis in this song on words that fall on the fourth beat as well.

Delay/Anticipate Melody

To play with the rhythm in your melody, you can try singing slightly before the beat, rather than exactly on it as the melody has been written. This creates anticipation by giving the song a pushed-forward feeling.

You can also drag the beat by singing just after the beat, giving it a lazier, dragged-out feeling.

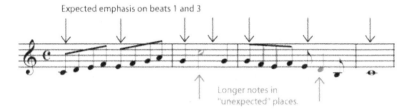

Try out all of these suggestions to keep your sense of rhythm on its toes!

EXERCISES

1) Using a song you've explored in earlier chapters, listen for: a) accented beats by various instruments, b) the groove, c) any "swing" feel, d) syncopation, e) musical articulation.

2) Using the same song, fill in the chart below indicating the time signature of the piece for both verse and chorus, the instruments used in the verse and chorus, and how the syncopation is used. I've included an example (Michael Jackson's "The Way You Make Me Feel") as a guide:

RHYTHMIC ELEMENT:	Beat Accents		Groove/Feel/ Swing		Syncopation/ Articulation	
SONG STRUCTURE:	Verse	Chorus	Verse	Chorus	Verse	Chorus
The Way You Make Me Feel - Michael Jackson	2 & 4	2 & 4	Drums, bass and synth line swing, forward moving.	same swing as verse	not much	Accents weaker beats with words at end of phrases

11. INTONATION

Goals: Understand how the most common issues limit your ability to sing on pitch, and have solutions to fix them.

Why? If you experience difficulty singing on pitch, it can limit your ability to stay in tune with the essence of your song. Understanding the root causes of pitch issues can make the experience of your voice significantly better.

. . . .

The human voice is not always immediately available perfectly on pitch. It can take months, even years, of training before a singer is able to maintain accurate pitch consistently. Remember, most modern audiences are not formally musically trained, but their exposure to high quality recordings is vast. They may not be able to tell you what exactly is wrong with a weak singer, but nearly everyone can identify a singer singing either out of rhythm or out of pitch, even if only slightly. It is very important both for your own enjoyment and for your future audience that you learn how to identify and correct any pitch issues.

Singing "On The Note"

When a guitar player tunes her guitar, she must align the pitch of one string to another until all strings resonate together in harmony. She does this by adjusting the strings either sharp (slightly above) or flat (slightly below) until they resonate correctly.

Vocalists must learn to do the same thing. You must learn how to tune your voice not above or below the intended note, but directly on it. You must learn how to sing like this on every pitch. But that can be challenging in various ways for various reasons. In this chapter we take a closer look at these.

Voice-Habits

Remember that your ultimate goal as a developing singer should be to keep your voice free of unintentional strain. By understanding your voice habit and common solutions for these habits (see earlier chapters), you can break free of your habit and perfect your pitching in these difficult areas of the voice.

If you still experience difficulty singing in those areas (for example, your voice suddenly becomes breathy in tone, experience strain, hoarseness, cracks or breaks, or any general unease), then make sure you seek a vocal professional who can correctly balance your critical bridge seamlessly together to make one strong-sounding voice with no breaks or strain.

Slow Down

One of the most overlooked solutions when experiencing difficulties with singing on pitch is simply to slow down your practice! If you're singing a scale and having trouble, slow down in the tricky area and establish exactly where in the scale your pitch is going off key. In the majority of cases, make sure you address the tendencies of your voice-habit. If you are experiencing strain, you may require some vowel tuning solutions (see chapter five on The Sweet Spot).

When singing your songs, if you are singing along to a recording make sure you stop the recording and work through the lyric one phrase at a time looking for the problematic area. Isolate the area that is throwing you off pitch, and work through that area very slowly. Try to establish what is causing the note to go off pitch. Are you above or below the intended pitch? If you are not sure, record yourself and listen back. What do you need to change to get the note onto the correct pitch?

Once you have established what you need to correct the pitch, very gradually over a few minutes (or longer) try to build your way back up to the regular speed. Just don't go any faster than you can handle while staying on pitch!

Listening

Another common issue is that the singer can become so wrapped up in the message of the lyric they are singing or the experience of the song in general that they forget to listen to the music itself - specifically, they forget to listen to their reference of certain instruments to stay on pitch with the melody. Be careful you don't get so caught up in your emotional experience that you forget to listen to and align your voice with the actual music!

The Melody's Tonal Center

If you struggle with maintaining pitch it's helpful to find the melody's "tonal center". This is the place that all the notes in the melody revolve around, leave from, and go back to. It creates a point of reference in your mind as you sing your melody.

Most melodies have as their tonal center the tonic, or the first degree (note) of the song's scale or key. You can quickly work out what note that is by searching for the key of the song you are singing on a search engine. The tonic will be the same note as the key of the song. For instance, if the key of the song is in A major, the tonal center for the melody will likely be the A note. If you have access to a keyboard (there are many free, digital ones online) and hit the A either below or above middle C, you will notice how the melody of the song seems to revolve around that pitch. Holding that pitch squarely in your mind will give you a strong reference point for your singing and improve your ability to stay on pitch.

Level of Difficulty

If you experience pitch issues that are not related to your coordination of your critical bridge or your awareness of the music it's likely that you have chosen a song with a melody that has difficult intervals or other complex musical elements. In that case, you should choose a song with a simpler melody, or do some basic interval training, explored in the next section.

Intervals

The distances between notes in a melody change constantly in songs. Often when singing from one note to another, we may not sing the spaces or distances between them exactly right, causing us to "miss" the note. Missing a note, even slightly, can be difficult to bear in modern singing. To help us with this dilemma, it's helpful to hone your skill in identifying and singing intervals in music so you can refine your ability to be more precise with the notes you sing.

An interval in music is a combination of two notes played either together or in sequence (one after the other). The distances between notes are the building blocks of melody. In western music, we distinguish the different possibilities of intervals by their quality (major, minor, diminished, or augmented) and number (unison, second, third, fourth, etc), and whether the notes are in ascending or descending order. Common intervals that are used in melodies are minor thirds and major thirds, for instance.

Nursery rhymes can have repeating intervals that are easy to grasp. For example, in the beginning of the nursery rhyme "Frere Jacques", the intervals ascending are spaced out by seconds, before dropping a third back to the beginning again (see the chart below). Having a better understanding of intervals can help you to sing with greater precision.

Without going too much into music theory, it's important to begin to build an understanding of how intervals in music sound in songs. This can take some practice and time, so allow yourself some time practicing identifying the differences. For more help with exploring intervals check out some of the many fantastic resources available online, such as musictheory.net

Interval Characteristics

Don't get disappointed if in the beginning most intervals sound similar. That's normal. Instead, try to focus on the subtle qualities of the intervals. What characters do they have? Certain intervals are quite common and occur frequently in many melodies, so in the beginning it's helpful to try and recognize the character of the sounds of the intervals.

Consonance & Dissonance

No concept is more important to western music than that of consonance and dissonance. These qualities alone are responsible for the power of music to create a sense either of rest or of tension and movement.

Consonance: Consonant intervals are stable and do not require resolution to another note. When an interval is consonant, it has a sense of rest about it, as if there isn't really anywhere else to go. There's no sense of being pulled in any direction.

Dissonance: By contrast, dissonant intervals are tense and do require resolution. They are more active. They create a sense of being pulled in a particular direction: either up or down, away from the note that is being played. They want to resolve into consonant notes.

Practicing Intervals

The table on the next page lists all the variations of intervals and gives examples of songs which use them, so you can hear what they sound like. The first words or notes of the songs listed in the boxes are examples of the corresponding intervals on the left. If you are not familiar with the song, dig it up on Youtube and learn them. Practice the interval by holding the first note of the interval for two beats and hold the second note of the interval for two beats, and repeat. See if you can make the changes more accurate and more quickly.

Interval	Ascending	Descending
Minor second (Dissonant)	Jaws theme song A Hard Days Night (Beatles) Stormy Weather (Arlen/ Koehler)	Für Elise (Beethoven) Joy To The World Shall We Dance (The King and I)
Major second (Dissonant)	Silent Night; Do-Re-Mi (Sound of Music) Rudolph The Red-Nosed Reindeer Frère Jacques	Yesterday (Beatles) Mary Had a Little Lamb Three Blind Mice The First Noël
Minor third (Consonant)	So Long, Farewell (Sound Of Music) Oh Canada Bad (Michael Jackson) Oh Where, Oh Where Has My Little Dog Gone	Hey Jude (Beatles) Frosty The Snowman This Old Man Misty (Erroll Garner)
Major third (Consonant)	Kumbaya Morning Has Broken Oh When the Saints	Summertime Man In the Mirror Swing Low Sweet Chariot
Perfect fourth (Consonant or Dissonant)	Amazing Grace Here Comes The Bride Love Me Tender (Elvis Presley)	Oh Come all ye faithful Born Free (John Barry)
Tritone (Dissonant)	"The Simpsons" theme song Maria (West Side Story)	Blue Seven (Sonny Rollins)
Perfect fifth (Consonant)	Twinkle Twinkle Little Star Star Wars Theme song Scarborough Fair Can't Help Falling In Love (Elvis Presley)	It Don't Mean a Thing (Duke Ellington) Feelings (Richard Clayderman) Have You Met Miss Jones
Minor sixth (Consonant)	She's a Woman (Beatles)	Please Don't Talk to Me When I'm Gone
Major sixth (Consonant)	My Bonnie Lies Over The Ocean My Way (Frank Sinatra) Angels (Robbie Williams)	Nobody Knows the Trouble I've seen The Music of The Night (Phantom of the Opera) Man In The Mirror (Michael Jackson)
Minor seventh (Dissonant)	Somewhere (West Side Story) Star Trek Theme	Lady Jane (Rolling Stones)
Major seventh (Dissonant)	Take Me On (A-Ha) Don't Know Why (Norah Jones)	I Love You (Cole Porter)
Octave (Consonant)	Somewhere Over The Rainbow (Wizard Of Oz) I'm Singing In The Rain	Willow Weep For Me

Remember that the degree to which you've been able to re-balance your voice-habit will directly effect how accurately and easily you can sing intervals, especially intervals which are wider apart (fifth, sixth, etc). That's because wider intervals can challenge you to shift from one register of your voice into another, because they cover a wider range of your voice. If you don't allow the shift to occur, you may find that your voice will become breathy in tone, break, crack or strain. If this happens to you, give your voice a rest, and try to use only the sounds suggested for your voice habit in the chapter on voice habits.

Computer Guidance

Studies have shown that real time visual feedback when learning correct pitching dramatically improves a singer's ability to sing on pitch. A great program you can use to accompany you in this chapter is the visual feedback software "Sing And See" (www.singandsee.com). This will help you establish whether you are flat or sharp of a note you intend to sing, and will greatly enhance your ability to be accurate with your pitches.

There are also many great online programs that will teach you this for free. Some good ones are www.good-ear.com, www.earmaster.com, and www.risingsoftware.com/auralia.

If you get stuck working with these programs, do the exercises below, which explore the sound of intervals in actual melodies of songs. Then you can return to more practice with the online tools.

Recording Yourself

After you have gained some familiarity practicing your intervals, record yourself and listen back to be sure you are shifting as precisely as possible. You will learn much more about your voice too!

EXERCISES

1) If you are experiencing pitch issues, what characteristics do your pitch issues have? Are you usually sharp (just above the intended note) or flat (just below your intended note)? Do you think these problems are because of: your voice-habit, your musicianship, or a lack of listening to the music?

_____

2) Are there certain intervals which you find more challenging than others? Which ones? How can you incorporate them into your practicing?

_____

THE VOCAL
PERSONALITY
IMPULSE

"Style is primarily a matter of instinct."

- BILL BLASS

12. YOUR NATURAL VOCAL TIMBRE

Goals: Be aware of the unique and aesthetic qualities of your natural voice.

Why? Often, when beginning singers hear their voices played back to them for the first time, they are shocked! Learning about the natural timbre of your voice allows you to have more perspective about your voice so you can envision your songs more accurately.

. . . .

Remember that you may still be developing your voice to coordinate across your complete range for singing to sing in a natural, relaxed, and healthy way. It can take time to skillfully coordinate your full range with a good degree of ease and creativity. When listening back to your voice, remember these things and make sure that you are gentle with yourself, accepting your voice in this context. Accept its weaknesses of balance - they are temporary. Instead, be attentive to its subtleties of tone and anything else that makes it distinctive in a positive way. These will be the qualities that you will build on as you seek to bring out the unique and distinctive character and personality in your voice.

> "Finding the true natural voice is the key to healthy singing; the rest is a question of style."
>
> - OREN L. BROWN

Listening Beyond Your Imperfection

You must be extremely gentle with yourself as you begin to listen to your voice. In the beginning of training, since your voice may not always be perfectly tuned, it can be difficult to hear yourself sing off pitch, or hear your voice strained or imperfect in any way. Try to listen beyond the imperfections and attune to its unique qualities. The point of this is to have a budding awareness of your unique tonal qualities. Let the seed of your understanding of your unique natural timbre plant itself. Be gentle, not critical, with your voice.

Separating Influences

We gain extraordinarily and invaluably from observing, listening, and admiring our vocal influences. Indeed, the idols that inspire us to sing can ignite deep reservoirs of inspiration that can help to weather the sometimes long process of vocal development. But when it's time to discover your unique natural qualities, you have to set aside the fascinating qualities of the voices of those you are influenced by. Instead, you must learn to observe, listen, and admire your own voice - with an open mind and an open heart.

This can be difficult. We may feel so in awe of the seeming vocal perfection of our idols that we become immensely critical of our own imperfections, unable to hear our own voice for what it naturally is. If you find this happening to you (and it happens to some degree to all of us), have comfort knowing you are not alone. Remember that the Singer's Instinct requires that you be attentive to your own impulses. If you can't escape the sound of your idol's voices running through your head, you simply can't be attentive to the subtle signals of your instinct.

Similarly, when the voices of your influences distract you from your own singing style, your voice can take on a fake, inauthentic tone and/or style. If this happens, quiet your mind and return to your own relaxed, natural vocal production, just as if you were speaking. Connect with the sensations of your singing: the way your breathing feels as you inhale/ exhale; the way your vocal cords and larynx feel as you sing; the way your amplifier adjusts to form vowels and consonants. Try to tune in to every sensation of your singing, as subtle as these may seem. As you begin to form a conscious connection with the qualities of your natural timbre, every sensation and vocal quality counts. All can become fascinating seeds for experimentation and exploration later.

Vocal Timbre Versus Classification

It's important to distinguish between the qualities that are unique in your voice and voice classifications such as bass, baritone, tenor, alto, soprano etc. Many singers haven't learned how to access their full range correctly, and thus may get the idea that they belong to an inappropriate voice classification (for instance, many baritones and altos are undeveloped and misclassified tenors and sopranos). Furthermore, these conventional voice classifications don't necessarily have much relevance to contemporary music, where the expectation to explore and be original is much greater.

Although voice classifications are important in some genres of music, in this chapter we're concerned with something deeper - the actual sound qualities of your natural vocal timbre. This can take some time to learn.

"Is That REALLY me?"

We can live our whole lives before we realize the sound of our own voice is not what we thought it was! That's because the vibrations our ears pick up in our head is not what the world hears - it's only what we feel.

It has been said there are three voices that we ultimately experience:

1) The voice we FEEL inside our head and body
2) The voice we THINK our audience hears in our speaking/singing

3) The voice our audience ACTUALLY hears

The first two experiences are inaccurate and misleading but common. Understanding what your audience actually hears, however, is crucial to maximizing your vocal potential.

Effects & Altering Timbre

You will find in time that your voice is naturally suited for certain kinds of music and vocal demands, but that doesn't mean you can't experiment with various vocal effects and your natural timbre. Many singers have become masterful at enhancing their natural timbre by employing fresh effects to create distinctive singing styles. British vocalists in particular seem to be quite adept at this. Singers such as Amy Winehouse, Adele, Lily Allen and a few others have capitalized on a textually lazy quality to their singing, giving their natural timbres the unique twist of being almost emotionally distant, even defiant. The trick is to find your unique sound through experimental trial and error, through your continuous, deliberate practice (more on practicing techniques in chapter 16).

Nasality

If you hear elements of nasality in certain ranges of your voice, it means that there is too much air resonating the nasal cavities. This may be because the velo-pharyngeal port (the flap that dangles from your hard palette) is not working correctly to expose enough of your mouth, or it may mean that your larynx has risen too high and is affecting your velum, pulling your tongue too far back, or creating other imbalances. In both cases, it can be enough to tune problematic words/vowels with a deeper larynx (see The Sweet Spot chapter). Then work in your speaking range to master the coordination between a healthy sounding spoken vowel sound and an exaggerated nasal vowel sound with the same vowel. What do you feel changes in your mouth? Can you master that change for higher pitches?

Exercises

1) Listen to a recording either of one of your voice lessons or of yourself singing a simple verse of a song with an easy dynamic in a comfortable part of your range. What qualities come to mind? Don't get stuck on labels or words here - just listen with an open mind and learn to hear your voice as it truly is. Are you reminded of other vocalists? Why?

_____

_____

2) Do you hear your voice as having a deep timbre, or a lighter sweeter timbre? Somewhere in between?

_____

_____

13. Riffs & Embellishments

Goals: Add riffs and embellishments tastefully, without using too many or overshadowing the main melody.

Why? A good modern singer occasionally adds embellishments on the spot, whenever they feel the urge stemming from their emotional engagement with the song. Understanding and adding vocal embellishments will make your vocals sound more authentic and exciting.

. . . .

In contrast to holding out a note straight in a melody, vocal embellishments add quick pitch variations of a few notes immediately above and/or below the original note. You can add ornamentation to the melody at any point to make it more interesting and to give it a sense of beauty. Because it can take time to sing riffs with a good degree of accuracy, you should first aim to be able to accurately produce simple trills, and gradually build towards longer riff phrases with more complex patterns.

A singer with a good instinct is able to fully stay with the original melody while providing just enough variation to keep it interesting and fresh. Too many embellishments and you will lose the authenticity of the moment. Too much embellishment also ruins the opportunity to enjoy the original melody. But if you don't use enough variation, the song won't have any sense of surprise. Done tastefully, embellishments are like brush strokes in the sky: they take your singing into the stratosphere through their wild, complex melodic patterns and precise pitches, which are experienced as sophisticated emotional expression!

The best way to learn how to add ornaments to the melody is to study the singers you love as they do it. Try to discern what the original, or simplified, version of their melody is, and what they did to ornament that.

> **"Before I sing, I must feel."**
>
> - IRA D. SANKEY

Pentatonic Scale

The majority of embellishments are based on the pentatonic scale, which only uses 5 of the 7 degrees of the major scale: degrees 1, 2, 3, 5 and 6 (4 and 7 are left out). Using only these notes, and skipping the fourth and seventh, creates a very bluesy and sophisticated effect.

The diagram below shows the notes that would be played on the pentatonic scale in the key of C major. The degrees of each note in this key would be: C (1), D (2), E (3), G (5), A (6), C (1). The diagram uses arrows to show which keys on the keyboard you would skip. Between C and D, for instance, there is a distance of a full tone, but the distance between E and G is a tone and a half, or a "tone-plus":

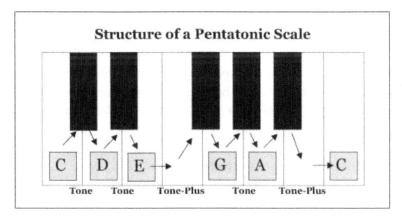

In the key of A, the pentatonic notes would be: A (1), B (2), C# (3), E (5), F# (6), A (1). In the key of F# major, the pentatonic scale would encompass only the black keys of the keyboard: F# (1), G# (2), A# (3), C# (5), and D# (6).

General Embellishment Guidelines

The embellishment exercises in the next section will help you become aware of any build-up of inappropriate tension in the voice. All these tricks take time to learn how to do precisely, quickly, and easily, but if you bear the following guidelines in mind, you should be able to build up gradually to your own creative riff patterns:

- Be careful you don't overwhelm yourself with all the notes at once by focussing on what the result of the riff should sound like. Instead, focus on executing the riff by mastering each note on its own, then in sequence with each other, slowly at first. Take your time and make sure you are outlining each pitch in the riff precisely. Allow yourself to fully internalize the riff before you try speeding it up to the speed the artist uses.

- Keep the rhythms of your riffs simple until you master the notes, then add some subtle variations such as holding one or two notes in the middle of a riff. Keep your changes small until you learn how to create nuances with your riffs. Ultimately, remember, you want your riffs to indicate how you feel about the music and the lyric, not be just for the sake of doing them.

Your ability to make the runs faster will improve naturally over time. Don't try to force it, or your your melody will sound hazy and messy. Remember, every note must be clearly produced for embellishment effects to work. Only go as fast as you can while producing every pitch cleanly.

Note Trill

The trill is created by going back and forth to and from the original note in either direction 3 or 4 times. You can lick back and forth from the original note of a melody at any point of the phrase to the pitch either above or below it on the pentatonic scale in the key of the song.

In the key of G major, for instance, the pentatonic notes are G, A, B, D, and E. So if the the note you want to embellish is A, you

could sing either from A to the B right above it and back, or to the G below it. If the note you want to trill from is B, you could sing to either the D above or the A below.

Tail-Lick

When you drop or ascend from an ending note of a phrase in a melody, it creates a "tail" effect. This kind of lick adds only 1 or 2 notes descending or ascending quickly from the last note of a phrase. This kind of lick can have the feeling of a question being asked. Although it is usually done at the end of a phrase, it can be creatively added not just to the ends of phrases but anywhere in the midst of a phrase as well. Jessie J makes an impressive upward lick at the beginning of her song with the last word "free" at the end of her first sentence "I'm feeling sexy and free".

The numbers below represent the degrees in the pentatonic scale that could be tail-licks. Some are ascending from the original note (as in the first and third), and some are descending (as in the second and fourth). So, for example, you might sing the following note changes:

- 1-2
- 6-5
- 1-2-3
- 5-3-2

Drop-Lick

You can create a more dramatic lick from the ends of phrases with a run of 4 or 5 notes either up or down. In Mariah Carey's "Hero" she makes a drop of two notes at the last word of the first line in the 2nd verse "It's a long road":

- 1-2-3-5
- 1-6-5-3-2

You can also create a "U" shape by dropping down 2, 3 or 4 notes then coming back up to the original note. We hear an example of this at the beginning of the Boyz II Men song "It's So Hard To Say Goodbye To Yesterday" on the word "I" in "How do I say goodbye..."

- 5-3-2-3-5-6-5
- 1-6-5-3-2-3-6-5

Remember, having too many licks can weaken their effect. You need just enough to maintain interest and a feeling of surprise.

Down/Upward Spiral

Added sophistication can be added by temporarily reversing the direction of a 4 or 5 note run halfway through and then back again. For instance, you could start a descent of 4 notes, go up two more, and down another 4 notes. In Mariah Carey's "Hero" she does this spiraling in the first verse on the last word in the phrase "and the sorrow that you know will melt away". This creates a wonderful sophisticated looping spiral effect:

- 5-3-2-3-2-1-2-1-6-5-6-1-2

Rhythmic Nuances

Sophistication of embellishments can also be achieved through bending (sliding from one pitch to another) or by holding certain notes in a series. By syncopating the rhythms of your riff, that is, by slightly dragging or pushing certain rhythms, holding one note briefly before quickly rushing through another group of notes, you can create rhythmic surprise and add a level of sophistication that is fascinating to listen to. Study how the singers you love do this and master their nuances.

Sustaining Notes

This is the opposite to licks and runs, but often just as powerful. By holding a note over the music, perhaps where a listener might least expect it, you create an intense and steady emotional state and can convey a very high degree of dramatic tension. For example, holding the fifth degree in the song's key at a strategic or well-planned point in the song's melody creates a powerful pull-effect in the music.

As an advanced exercise, see if you can get your band to stop time and hold a chord at the song's big moment as you hold your note. You just might tear the place apart when you come back to the rhythm to finish the song!

Be Inventive, But Don't Overdo It

As you get better with embellishing notes you can experiment with varying the rhythm or dynamic of the melody line too. The important thing is that you learn a variety of ways to indulge the original melody without getting too carried away. At all times, remember what your artistic intention is and what unique interpretation you will bring to the piece. Most importantly, let your instinct guide you. You will feel far more excited by your genuine feel for the song.

EXERCISES

1) Practice basic trills by singing back and forth between two notes in a comfortable part of your range. Start slowly and gradually pick up the pace. If you lose the precision of the notes, slow it down until you gain back the precision of your pitches.

2) Using a song you admire, see if you can pinpoint 1 or 2 licks that have similar structures to some of the licks described in this chapter. How are they different or similar?

_____

_____

3) Try singing the same line as above, but this time add a different lick in place of the on the recording. Where else in the music can you add similar effects?

_____

_____

14. Vocal Style

Goals: Allow your personality to come through in your singing by learning techniques for producing various dynamics.

Why? Singing with an easy dynamic is a great start, but eventually you need to learn how to build your voice so it can handle more varied dynamics to suit your emotional fancy or the song. A flexible vocalist should be able to sing softly, gently, or breathily to a full, strong belt and everything in between. All of these add colorful degrees of tension.

. . . .

I n the chapter on song analysis, we looked at how thoughts are broken down and expressed in musical phrases. A lot can happen in the thoughts of a singer in the course of even just one verse! In learning how to interpret a song, you're really learning to allow your unique thoughts and experiences about the music and lyrics you are singing to emerge, often in subtle ways.

Singing authentically means not copying the exact interpretation of songs from the singers you've modeled yourself after, but expressing your own Singer's Instinct. Become interested in what makes you special and what differences of personality and character you bring to the genre. As the vocalist, you are the central communicator of the music. You should know what the story that you are telling means to you, and have ways of engaging yourself more deeply in the story through whatever means inspire you at the time. Draw on what makes you unique, what makes you stand out. Learning some basic ways that you can interpret your song will empower you with more creative opportunities for your Singer's Instinct to emerge.

Respect Your Mistakes

Probably the most important skill to remember as you develop your own vocal style is how to make intelligent use of your mistakes. While we don't want to lock ourselves into detrimental voice-habits, making the odd mistake gives the sense that you're emotionally committed to your singing. Nearly every singer throughout time has managed to make their mistakes seem like irreplaceable elements of their unique vocal style. So as you develop your craft, have a growing awareness as you practice of whether the seemingly useless results of your vocal experimentation can provide the seeds for useful and interesting musical ideas.

Tone

Some of your most playful singing moments will come from your experimentation with your voice's unique tone - often through mistakes or discoveries. Although you want to keep your voice developing in the context of your voice-habit, you also want to allow yourself to discover the unique sounds that occur not just from a well balanced voice, but also from the moments in your singing where you experiment with the limits and sensations within each register. Remember, there is nothing wrong with the voice-habits themselves - they can provide the basis for some great sounds, and great varieties of tonality. There is everything wrong with the voice-habits, however, if you are stuck and can't break free of them.

Tone can be affected by:

- Vocal freedom (determined by your ability to sing easily from one area of your voice to another)
- Air pressure (excess air pressure created by your abdomen against your vocal cords causes your larynx to uncontrollably rise above a stable, appropriate position)
- The unique sound of your vocal cords and resonant cavities themselves, and how you adjust and control them
- The style, character, and genre of your song
- Your emotional engagement and requirements for the song
- Your personality!

Falsetto

In chapter 2 we discussed the various ways the voice produces sound, including falsetto. Falsetto is a kind of tonality, a function of the vocal cords usually due to an unbalanced voice, that produces an interesting vocal effect and can contribute to a singer's unique vocal style. For instance, after you have built some tension with a full high note, "flip" into falsetto. In effect you are dropping the tension of the note, as the normal tension in the voice gives out to a disconnected tone. Be careful, however, when using falsetto that you do not blow too much air, as this can aggravate the vocal cords and cause vocal problems.

Vocal Effects

The voice is capable of an endless array of sounds outside just words. Ray Charles and Bobby McFerrin are examples of singers who found ways to use their voices to create startling effects. "Mmm"s, cries, dramatic drops in pitch, microphone tricks, tongue flicks, even nonsense words can all be employed to create a more spontaneous and passionate delivery.

Other Effects

Perhaps you feel compelled to add a growl, a moan, a sigh somewhere in the words you are singing. Other ways to play are through being lazy or crisp with vowels and consonants, being breathy in tone, or any deviation from an easily produced vocal sound. Also, you could give any repeating melodic fragments in songs slight variations to keep the interest of the listener and imply a more authentic delivery.

Using Voice-Habits

Some very famous gospel singers such as Etta James were famous for their grinding vocals where they seemed to create a raspy vocal tone by attacking key notes hard, closing their vocal cords tightly, just as a strainer would do. The difference from a singer who can experiment with this voice-habit in a conscious way, and a singer who succumbs to this voice-habit unable to break free of it, however, is that one is free to experiment, and the other note. Each of the voice-habits can be explored in a healthy way as long as you are able to maintain a balanced voice in your practice.

> "Ray Charles's records disclose an extraordinary assortment of slurs, glides, turns, shrieks, wails, breaks, shouts, screams, and hollers, all wonderfully controlled, disciplined by inspired musicianship, and harnessed to ingenious subtleties of harmony, dynamics, and rhythm. He can't tell it to you. He can't even sing it to you. He has to cry out to you, or shout it to you, in tones eloquent of despair or exhalation."
>
> - HENRY PLEASANTS

Pitch Variation

You might feel certain words of a lyric resonate more with you at a given time, and so you might naturally feel like placing an emphasis on those words. You can take a word to a higher or lower pitch than is written, or accent a particular syllable, syncopating the rhythm, making it stand out more. Perhaps you actually speak a few words off the pitch, throwing off expectation.

By dragging or varying the melody you can change up the notes in verses and choruses, adding flair to repeating sections. Set up the melody the first time by keeping it simple. But after that, change it up!

Full Voice to Light Dynamic

Singing with wide dynamics is a highly advanced vocal skill: singing from a soft, gentle tone, to a fuller, more powerful sound without strain or disconnecting into falsetto. The ability to do this produces an array of vocal colors from breathy, light and angelic, to powerful and dramatic. Many gospel, soul and rock singers, such as Aretha Franklin, Etta James, James Brown, Steven Tyler and are known for their ability to wail at full, powerful sometimes distorted-sounding intensities.

Lyric/Melody Relationship

Most melodies are written to compliment the lyric, which is often sung with rhythmic and melodic inflections similar to how we would actually speak it. But there are many ways to accent how you sing your line to make it stand out and create a dramatic effect.

Emphasis

Your interpretation of a song will emerge primarily out of the emphasis and de-emphasis on key words you choose, in a way that is different from how others have provided their emphasis. You can use:

- Tonal variety such as falsetto, breathiness, full tones, and vocal effects
- Melodic variation and pitch changes
- Rhythmic and groove variations and pauses

Articulation

Listen to how the other instruments play and/or sing their phrases. How do they break up one phrase from another by grouping together successions of notes? How they phrase, and how you respond and/or add your own phrasing, provides an advanced sense of groove to the song and can help imbue the song with more feeling.

Simply singing a line more softly or more loudly can really draw attention to whichever aspect you change. Also, if a particular melodic motif is used frequently, as is often the case in popular music, adding small variations of dynamic is often enough to keep the song fresh, without adding too much melodic or rhythmic variety. When you use articulation to enhance the rhythmic nuances of the music, you really solidify the groove of the song.

Rhythmic Variation

Experiment with expectation by varying the melodic accents slightly: sing the melody a little off the beat by starting to sing either just before the beat it is expected to start on or just after it. See how that plays with expectation – it will build an alluring tension.

You can choose key moments in the lyric to drag out a note where one leasts expects it, or cut a note or two shorter than they are written. This can produce a great deal of emphasis on a particular word, and can greatly alter the melody line, since if you drag out the notes in a melody you may have words after that you will have to catch up with to finish the line on time with the rhythm. This creates exciting rhythmic variety. You may feel like dropping out a few words altogether, grunting, adding a new line, changing the melody: all of these impulses should be followed, developed and trusted.

Be Creative

Understanding the lyric of your song is crucial to being able to channel or communicate it. The meaning of a song and the lyric are always open to interpretation by the singer, but the most important thing is that you study how other great singers have phrased before you and borrow from their inspiration. The wonderful thing about music is that you can take as many liberties as you like, as long as they remain tasteful.

A song can be performed in an infinite variety of ways. The lyric could be heart wrenching, but you may choose to sing it joyfully or dispassionately. All of these variations are ways to experiment with your delivery that will eventually lend themselves to a unique vocal sound for you.

Be Careful!

These spontaneous effects keep things fresh for your singing. Just be careful you do not overuse them or get stuck in a badly produced voice coordination. Exciting, spontaneous singing requires lots of the right education and experience of using your unique instrument in order to keep your voice healthy and free enough to fully explore the possibilities it can offer. If you push it too far, it can create a host of vocal problems that can dramatically reverse your vocal abilities and take some time (and the skill of a very good teacher) to readjust.

> "Being able to act intelligently and instinctively in the moment is possible only after a long and rigorous education and experience."
>
> - MALCOLM GLADWELL

If you've taken particular liberties with experimenting with your voice, you might want to give your voice a rest altogether, or rebalance, or re-tune your voice back to a healthier condition with the right exercises for your voice-habit after singing. Developing expressivity with your voice in a healthy way is a skill that can take some time to develop well.

EXERCISES

1) Hold one note in a comfortable part of your range on one sound using vibrato. Gradually increase the dynamic or intensity of the note without ever straining, and then return to a medium dynamic. Finally, diminuendo (decrease the intensity as far as you can without getting a breathy tone). Can you keep a balanced voice?

_____

2) Sing a song you sang earlier in the book, applying some new effects from this chapter that you've never used before or that you don't use often. How does it enhance your singing?

_____

_____

3) Could you integrate the elements above that you particularly like more comprehensively into your own vocal style? What songs could you experiment with this on?

_____

4) Choose a song that has always inspired you or that you would like to perform. Why are you drawn to it? What are the melodic, rhythmic and lyric emphases in the song that draw you to it? What is your relationship to what you're singing about in the song you've chosen? Can you increase awareness of these in your singing?

_____

_____

5) What personal experiences, or what aspects of your personality, can be the basis for your own unique interpretation of the song? How can you reveal those aspects of your personality through the effects you use in the song?

_____

_____

15. INTUITIVE PHRASING

Goals: Be able to sing playfully with interesting and unique phrasing on your own, ideally without feeling self-conscious.

Why? The key to enjoying singing is being able to entertain yourself! A sense of playful phrasing can help keep you happy, give you a sense of fulfillment, and foster creativity.

. . . .

As Hollywood vocal coach Dave Stroud claims, most modern singing styles require that you sound natural and free, often even imperfect. In other words, the culture of modern singing means that often you will have to bend the rules to get the kind of modern sound you might be used to hearing. The challenge is to make sure that the aspects of your singing that are imperfect don't interfere with your vocal health by tiring your voice, creating strain, or becoming a habitual pattern that can entrap your voice, limiting your ability to sing freely or with a wide range in the long-term.

"Most styles will require that you bend the rules at least a little, some styles more than others. So the question is, how much can you "bend the rules" and have that be a temporary condition, rather than having it become a habit."

- DAVE STROUD

When singing, it's likely that you will find yourself concentrating on a whole number of things simultaneously, which is often why modern singers sound imperfect in the first place. Other instruments generally have only one sound that can be made on their various pitches. As singers, however, you have an entire catalogue of sounds that must be coordinated as correctly as possible on every pitch across your entire vocal register (even the awkward places in your voice). Because of the difficulty of transitioning between the low and high voice while coordinating a wide variety of sounds that engage your tongue, mouth cavities, and lips, singing the lyrics over the wide range of pitches that the melodies of a song typically require can be extremely difficult in the beginning of the singing process. Not only that, but your songs should be sung with emotion and musicality, that is, with a sense of your personality in the melody, just like other musicians.

Songs can be very challenging. Pitches and vowel changes occur quickly in the lyrics of the song, yet as a singer your pitch changes should be easy and precise. The dynamics of the melody may change frequently, the emotional intent can be overwhelming, or the song may have difficult passages that you struggle with. Make sure you take one thing at a time with your singing. Master one skill before moving on and attempting another - otherwise you won't know how to adjust your singing for maximum creativity. Remember your ultimate goal: to sing with a voice that is free of breaks and strain.

> "When we are learning to sing we cannot see or touch what we are working with... The unskilled performer invariably increases tension and effort. If the musculature of the larynx has been developed properly through training, this is not necessary."
>
> - INGO TITZE

The result in the beginning is that some part of your coordination will likely falter - and that's perfectly ok, as long as it doesn't create a buildup of tension vocally. As beginning modern singers, you can accept that you will not always sing with a perfected sound. The key is to maintain as much of a free voice as you can in your practicing (see the chapter on Practicing for tips on good practice techniques), find ways to enjoy your singing as is appropriate for your current vocal ability, while always working to improve your coordination, balance, and strength.

"If you want to have fun with your songs," I suggested to Luanne, who had been feeling trapped and unable to be expressive with her singing "practice your singing while you're distracted with more mundane tasks. Do it when you're driving, vacuuming, or even doing the dishes." When you focus too much on your singing, you can become self-conscious or trapped in your own patterns. By keeping your conscious mind busy, you allow your unconscious mind to engage with new skills, often bringing in inventiveness and fresh creativity.

Luanne came back the next week absolutely thrilled: "I decided to record myself while I was singing and doing the dishes," she said. "I did quite a few things I thought were quite interesting which I would never have done before." What Luanne had done was instinctively slowed down her singing because she was singing a capella (without music accompanying her). She began playing with the melodies unconsciously, pausing, slowing down, or speeding up randomly. She sang up rather than down, made wider jumps or smaller ones in her melody, and the emotion in her voice started to emerge spontaneously, rather than being forced or not showing up at all.

As singers, it's important to connect with this sense of play. For the purposes of singing, vocal play could be defined as:

- Allowing yourself to be silly
- Suspending your usual judgment towards yourself
- Carelessly allowing mistakes, successes, or whatever else arises
- Experimenting with learned skills
- Freely exploring what is unfamiliar
- "Purposefully creating without purpose", that is, singing in a genuinely open-minded, playful way, without an immediate agenda
- Reconnecting with a childhood sense of ease and openness

> "When you are playing for yourself, you discover the really good ideas that are inside of you."
>
> - ANONYMOUS MUSICIAN

Distract Yourself

Play is meant to be simple, spontaneous, and stress-free. Don't over-think it. The trick is to distract yourself as you do it. Find a way to keep your conscious mind engaged with mundane tasks: Driving, doing the dishes, in the shower or car, walking, admiring art, and cleaning are all fantastic opportunities to sing playfully. Let yourself let go, relax, and have fun.

Remember to record yourself so you don't forget what you did! You may discover some tricks you've forgotten or would not have thought of. You might also be surprised at how expressive and/or interesting your singing already is!

Staying Focussed

Although playful singing requires a sense of letting go, it also requires a sense of focus. Singing without any attention at all can become unmusical. It requires at least a basic attention to all of the elements you've studied previously. If you feel like you get off-track with any of the more basic elements of your singing (such as going off pitch or beginning to strain), ask yourself how you can adjust your singing so that you can be become free enough again to be playful with it.

> "Staying present is the discipline of play. Playful enterprises are alert. They are open to information, always seeking more, yearning for surprises."
>
> - WHEATLEY AND KELLNER-ROGERS

Avoid Comparing Yourself

It's important to accept your voice as and where it is at this moment. It's perfectly ok if you aren't as virtuosic in your abilities as some of the powerhouse vocalists you admire. Instead, foster an environment of relaxed confidence in your abilities as they are now, and be thankful for the unique opportunity to continue to develop your vocal skills.

Studying Other Musicians

A great way to learn how to have fun with your melodies is to listen to how other instrumentalists in jazz, blues, rock, and other genres play with their melodies to make them their own. For example, some of the best jazz singers in the world regularly studied saxophone players - and even Louis Armstrong admitted to singing the way he played his horn!

When you allow yourself to fulfill the inner urge of the simple vibrant passion of play, you engage a truly primal essence. As children, play was an essential aspect of your growth. It is essential to strengthening neural pathways in your brain, and to teaching you how to enjoy and stay engaged in the moment. Play can allow a significant part of what constitutes your individuality to surface, being a vital force to creative success. It creates an environment for you to express yourself freely, to learn about yourself, bringing you closer to the core of your Singer's Instinct.

EXERCISES

1) Find one opportunity in your week to experiment with play. Go watch children play in a schoolyard and take note of their freedom, ease, and spontaneity. What do you enjoy doing that encourages you to be spontaneous?

_____

_____

2) What strengths do you feel are most helpful in engaging you more closely with your Singer's Instinct? What do you think is your particular strength as a singer, that distinguishes you from others?

_____

_____

3) Do you ever feel inferior in your skills as a vocalist so much that it inhibits your ability to be playful with your songs? What affirmations can you create that support your pursuit of play rather than competition or comparison?

_____

_____

THE IMPULSE
OF WISE
PRACTICE

"I go by instinct. I don't worry about experience."

- BARBRA STREISAND

16. How To Practice

Goals: Use a 6-step practice process to create efficient practice strategies for the fastest and most effective improvements.

Why? Learning efficient practicing techniques can really speed up your growth as a singer. This chapter works best as a supplement to your coaching with your current teacher, providing you with perspective on various exercises and their effectiveness.

. . . .

W hen singers come into my studio hot on the heels of a new quest to develop their voices, they're often not exactly sure what they want from their training with me. It's important to understand your goals as a vocalist. What exactly are you trying to achieve with your practicing? Are you looking to just warm up your voice, or are to achieve specific goals for which you'll need to apply a specific workout for your voice-habit? Most singers have specific goals they are working towards. If that's the case for you, remain aware as you practice of whether or not you're improving towards your goals, and what changes you might be able to make to improve the quality of your practicing.

The Singer's Responsibility

As a singer, you are asking your tiny vocal cords to do a huge variety of gymnastics. Some of these skills might include:

- Shifting quickly and effortlessly from one vibration speed (pitch) to another beyond the pitch ranges in which you normally speak
- Singing accurately between continuously changing pitches with changing distances (intervals) between them
- Singing from one area of resonance (voice register) to another smoothly, without breaking, cracking, or straining
- Forming all kinds of combinations of vowels and consonants while resonant sensations are shifting
- Singing with different intensities, sometimes powerful ones, without strain
- Singing with emotion or awareness of the meaning in your lyric
- Keeping the voice-box (larynx) relatively stable without it rising up excessively and engaging the swallowing muscles;
- Keeping the vocal cords working efficiently without them coming apart or creating a breathy tone
- Doing all that for a long time – anywhere from 4 mins to a few hours either in rehearsal or performance!

Different genres have different expectations that require various levels of these abilities. Opera, musical theatre, gospel, and R&B are among the most demanding of dynamic contrasts, fast accurate sequences of notes, and range. Whichever genre you sing in, however, aim to have your voice working well enough that you can be free to express yourself through it as you require.

When you practice, you are really improving your ability to manage one, or a combination, of all of these things. You must learn to develop whichever coordination is weakest or most desired in your voice, through deliberate practice. Although any kind of practice is better than no practice, maximizing the benefits of your practicing will determine how quickly you improve.

Practice Environment

If possible, find a regular space to practice that you can make your own. It should be a space where you feel free to make mistakes without feeling self-consciousness at all. If you have access to a rehearsal space, that works great. You may have a room in your living space - or you may need to pad out a closet so that little sound travels when you're in there singing your heart out. Some singers, including myself, love singing in cars. Some companies allow you to rent cars by the hour quite cheaply if you don't own one. This allows you to have a daily routine - perhaps practicing your singing while doing some errands driving!

Also, consider creating a "Singer's Shrine" for yourself wherever you practice. This can be a few pictures that inspire your love for singing: perhaps it's a picture or two of some of your favorite idols. Or maybe it's a picture from the stage capturing the excitement of an audience. Anything to motivate you and remind of your passion for the art.

Below is a detailed 6-step practice process. Use it as the foundation for your daily practicing regime. Start slow: In the beginning of your training limit your entire practice session to 10 - 15 minutes in total, resting for a few hours or the rest of the day before attempting more singing. Over a month or two, gradually increase the length of your practicing sessions up to 20 - 30 minutes, and even longer in the long term, always being careful never to over-work your voice, and stopping your routine whenever you feel vocally tired. After explaining the five steps, I provide a chart that gives some common goals and ways the steps can be adapted for each of those goals.

1. Focus Goals

In his book "The Talent Code", Dan Coyle notes that some of the most dramatic improvements to high performance tasks comes to those who practice with a deep motivation for learning. What was the reason you wanted to learn singing? Is there a particular artist who inspires you to sing at your best? Have you always wanted to impress others and earn admiration from your singing? Whatever your reason, it is the seed and potential powerhouse behind your future success. Every time before you start your warm-up, take a moment to really think about your motivation for learning singing, and choose one goal that has some challenge, but is not overwhelming or too difficult, that you can work towards in your session. Hold it in your mind as you embark on your session.

You may also want to use this time to focus your mind and get into the appropriate mental state you will need for your session. Focus on your breathing here. Allow your mind to slow down it's processing and allow you to re-focus your attention to your body, your emotions, and your mental activity. How are you feeling? Is there tension in your body? Envision how you want your session to go from beginning to end. How do you want to feel during your session? How do you want to feel after? This is your chance to prepare yourself for everything psychologically so when you start singing you are fully prepared, exactly as you need to be.

2. Tuning Up

Wouldn't you love a great short warmup that you can do before you start singing songs? Not so fast! There's more to getting the voice ready for singing than just a quick warmup. You also need to get the resonances and musculature for EVERY vowel in your dialect tuned up, especially in some of the more difficult areas of your voice - something singers often overlook, preferring to jump right into songs instead. For some more advanced singers, spending much time tuning up your voice with more challenging exercises might not be necessary. It's possible that some singers are so experienced and well-coordinated with their voices that they only need to warm up the correct skills that are already deeply ingrained.

But singers this prepared for singing are few indeed. For the vast majority still working towards keeping an even, strong voice, just warming up won't be enough. Much as you would tune the guitar strings together for the guitar to sound its best, you will need to spend more time tuning up all of the registers of the voice together. Remember that there are over ten commonly used vowel sounds, and every one will require its own tuning, especially in higher ranges.

If you are just learning to balance your voice, invest at least ten minutes tuning up your voice for singing before you dive into song-work. As you start your tune up, begin by tuning up some of your more easy vowels from a comfortable range through your critical bridge on a few basic sounds that work for you. Ask yourself: do you need to be gentle on the vocal cords, or do you need to need to work a little harder to keep them closed so they don't come apart and become breathy-toned? Remember, just because your vocal cords come apart creating a breathy tone at a certain point doesn't mean you need vocal cord strengthening exercises. It's much more likely that you're straining in the transition between the low and high voice, so you may need to be gentler, not more aggressive. In general, aim to balance the transition between your low and high voice together without significant difficulties on most vowel sounds (e.g., "MUM", "GEE", "NO", "NAA", "NAY"). Refer to the chapters on Voice-Habits to find exercises that are good starting points for you. However, because singing songs requires the use of virtually every vowel and consonant, you must learn how to navigate all vowels and consonants within and between every register to have any good chance of using them in a song.

Though a skilled vocalist may only need a short amount of time to tune up their voice before a performance, untrained vocalists, especially singers with deeply ingrained voice-habits, commonly require much more time, maybe even months or longer, before they can sing in tune through their critical bridge without hurting themselves. Just as it takes time for a violinist to learn to play the full range of the violin in an engaging way, so too the human voice doesn't typically allow itself to stay tuned so easily if the resonant sensations and musculature of the vocal cords aren't first coordinated properly. Unlike all other instruments, the voice has to be tuned through your understanding and feel of the balance between your amplifier (vowel shape), breathing coordination, and closure of the vocal cords. Make sure you give your voice the chance it needs to become fully tuned up. When it comes to singing, it's the quality of your practice - how you do it - that counts more than how much you practice.

> "Your voice training should help you connect your voice through your entire range and help you negotiate the passage areas. You must never forget why you practice: You do so to set up the correct balance between your exhaled air on your vocal cords, allowing you to sing efficiently, and to then train your muscular system to live with that balance."
>
> - SETH RIGGS

In the long-term scheme of your practicing, work through the development of your voice, loosely following the guidelines below:

1. Transition easily through your critical bridge on a few vowel sounds that are comfortable for your voice-habit, using longer scales of more than an octave.

2. Transition with all vowels sounds through your critical bridge using longer scales of more than an octave.

3. On a few vowel sounds that are comfortable for your voice-habit, remain within your newly developed range or critical bridge, using scale patterns that repeat notes within your more challenging areas.

4. On all vowel sounds, remain within your newly developed range or critical bridge, using scale patterns that repeat notes within your more challenging areas.

5. Sustain with vibrato on a few vowel sounds that are comfortable for your voice-habit.

6. Sustain with vibrato on all vowel sounds.

As you begin your tune-up, first get the blood flowing into the vocal cords in an easy way to get them working. You can do a lip or tongue trill, or a hum. If you are without a pitch reference it's perfectly ok. You don't even particularly need a scale, although using one is certainly best for a warm up as it will start to deliberately align your voice with specific pitches. Slide from your low voice up into your high voice and back down again, feeling your voice as you go. Remember, every day is a new day with your voice, so feel out what it needs as you begin your warm up. What feels easy today? What feels more challenging? As always, remain aware of your voice's needs as your progress through your practice session.

3. Workouts

Once you have your voice tuned up consistently with some flexibility through as well as above and below your critical bridge, it doesn't necessarily mean you have the stamina to sing consistently in that way for the long amount of time required when singing a song. Without adequate conditioning, your voice can grow tired and lose its balance easily after singing for just a minute or two. If it's a more challenging song, you may not even make through the first chorus!

To condition your voice, you will need a workout of between 10 - 30 minutes, depending on your requirements. Performing vocalists will need to invest in longer workout periods to build stamina for the long performances required onstage. As you practice, be attentive to any changes in your voice, and avoid overworking it with exercises that create excessive challenges. You don't want to tire your voice before you start singing songs!

Working out your voice is exactly like working out your body at the gym. Find a balance of a series of exercises that use sounds and scale patterns that are easier for your voice-habit and sounds and scale patterns that provide you with some challenge. A balance of exercises and how you execute them is very important. Easy exercises for your voice-habit are like low intensity exercises at the gym while more challenging exercises are higher intensity exercises. Just like the gym, you don't want too much of one or the other but rather a nice balance that oscillates regularly and appropriately between the two to get the most buildup of stamina. Too much ease and your voice won't be building any conditioning. Too much challenge and your voice won't be able to maintain a good, balanced tuning, and will grow tired quickly.

There are some great customized workouts for every voice-habit on VocalizeU for the iPad that do all this and more. After leading you through a patented voice assessment process, this app assigns you a vocal workout of about 20 minutes that will put you on the right track to maintaining your voice's tuning for long periods of time.

4. Song-Work

After tuning up, spend about 10 minutes working through one song. A good way to get started with all your songs, particularly if you're struggling, is to remove the lyrics entirely and instead sing the melody on a sound that is comfortable for you from your vocal workouts, to help you establish and maintain a balanced voice. By getting rid of the lyrics and using one sound, you make it easier to relieve any difficulties you may be experiencing with the words. Once you've tried one sound, try a few others, ensuring that you maintain an even voice free of breaks and strain in your melody.

As you work through the lyrics, you may discover problematic words. Notice which is the word, or the first word (if there are a number of difficult ones), that causes you to trip up and lose your coordination. Stop singing the melody, identify where the note is on a keyboard, and work out the issue with that note as the focus, using a scale pattern on one of the vowel and sound combinations that is appropriate for your voice-habit. Once you've worked out the problem, return to the melody and see if you can keep the same feeling as when you sang the note correctly on the exercise. Refer to the chapter on voice-habits for more solutions.

As you work through your melodies and lyrics, decide what other aspects of your singing you'd like to improve. You may choose to develop your understanding of the song's structure, its melody over time, holding notes with vibrato or adding embellishments, or plan in other ways how you want your song to sound.

5. Sing!

Spend 5 minutes singing your song uninterrupted from beginning to end. Your goal in this segment of your practicing is to learn to multi-task the elements you are working on in your development at the same time as you sing without stopping. This is where your practicing should really come together and demonstrate your hard won efforts. Don't forget to enjoy your singing!

If you can, record yourself and listen back. Note what you did well and how it felt, and learn more about the difficult passages that you may be struggling with. See if you can identify what specific word, note, or series of either was the root culprit in causing problems. Refer to the appropriate section in this book for solutions. Once you've run one song through, you can go back and work through elements of the song once more before giving it another shot at singing it straight through, start back at step four with a new song, or go back to step two or three to work through more exercises developing an even stronger balance in your voice.

6. Review

Towards the end of your practice, or after you've had time to recover your energy from performance, spend a few minutes reviewing your practice session and note a few things that went well and one or two things that you can do to improve your practice for the future. Keep it simple and brief. Make a note of these things in your journal so it's ready for you to keep in the forefront of your mind when you begin to focus your goals when you focus your goals at your next session!

General Practice Guidelines

Depending on your needs as a singer, you may need more attention in certain areas rather than others. If you are struggling with balance in your voice, for instance, you may need to spend the majority of your practice time, if not all of it, tuning up your voice. Alternatively, if you're preparing for a recording, you may need to spend more time in song-work, working through the specifics of your songs, preparing you to stay reasonably balanced before you sing them. If you are preparing for a performance, depending on how close you are to the date, you may want to focus entirely on singing all of your songs straight through without stopping to recreate the actual performance experience as closely as possible. Feel out your voice out as you practice, and be attentive to what it needs.

The following practice chart outlines various alternatives for a typical 30 minute practice session (although you can apply a similar ratio for shorter or longer sessions) for some common goals listed on the left. The numbers indicate the number of minutes you might want to spend at each step for that goal. For the beginning singer, the focus is to get their voice conditioned for the demands of singing, so there is an emphasis on the workout step. For a singer looking to develop their voice for range, power, and/or ease, more emphasis should be placed on the finer details of tuning-up their voice. For recording preperation, more emphasis should be placed on song-work and creative interpretation. Prepping for a performance requires more emphasis on longer workouts (step 3), but if you're practicing on the actual day of a performance, you'll want to emphasize a longer goal focussing component, or preparing psychologically for your performance. Maintaining your voice will require a relatively even split between working out your voice in nearly equal proportions.

Goal	1. Focus Goals	2. Tune Up	3. Work Out	4. Song Work	5. Sing	6. Review
Beginner	3	5	15	0	5	2
Development (range, power, ease)	3	15	0	10	0	2
Recording Prep	3	10	0	15	0	2
Performance Prep	3	0	10	0	10	7
Pre-Performance	10	0	10	0	5	5
Maintenance	0	0	15	10	8	2

17. OPTIMAL SONGS, KEYS & RANGE

> **Goals:** Know how to identify the right song for you to sing, and if and how you should adjust the song's key.
>
> **Why?** Covering songs is a great way to build your ability, style and instinct as a vocalist. But picking the right song can be tricky. Understanding how to go about this process effectively can boost your confidence, creativity, and vocal ability.

. . . .

I first started working with a client - let's call him Mike - when he was experiencing great fatigue with his voice. He had previously been diagnosed with vocal nodules from incorrect singing habits, but some vocal rest had allowed him to recover most of his vocal health. As with most rock singers, Mike had spent most of his singing experience as a strainer, trying to reach up for the high notes with the feeling of the low notes, not realizing that he wasn't allowing the resonance and musculature to shift away from his low voice in his high ranges. We spent a great deal of time re-balancing his upper ranges so he could begin to experience some ease up there. When he left the studio after his lessons, he would feel more confident about his abilities.

Yet nearly every week he would return to the studio frustrated. Why did he sound great at the studio, but then over the course of the week after his lesson everything would gradually fall apart? Why did his buddies who were performing night after night onstage not have any problems, while he seemed to have so many and wasn't performing at all?

In his heart, Mike is a dedicated performer. I had assumed that Mike was spending half his time using exercises to maintain balance in his voice, and the other half trying on a few mild rock songs. What I didn't realize was that Mike's typical practice session was actually incredibly different. Mike would spend some time getting his voice tuned-up, yes, but then he would spend the overwhelming majority of his time attempting some of the most rigorous rock songs in rock history for hours at at time! Not only that, but he was trying to emulate their gritty, strained vocal qualities!

Mike was a huge fan of a very prominent rock singer in the '90s, whose voice was a dream for aspiring rock singers. The rock star seemed to have mastered the rasp that many singers are now fond of. "How does he do it?" Mike would ask. "How does he get that gritty sound?"

The rock star's grittiness came with a sacrifice of being unable to access his high voice, but most importantly it came at the expense of even being able to sing on pitch. While this rock star's studio versions of his songs were on pitch, his live versions were anything but! The rock star was so deeply rooted in pulling the feeling of his low notes up into his high notes, he couldn't get through a single song in his live sets without falling painfully off pitch a dozen times. What Mike didn't realize was that the rasp the rock singer was known for wasn't so much a vocal effect as a last ditch effort to stay on pitch after a considerable amount of ongoing strain - he was unconsciously and continuously lifting the feeling of the low voice as high as he could take it, which was the root of his highly-prized rasp! This rock star sang in this way song after song, year after year, so it's no wonder that he struggles to sing on pitch in his live performances to this day. As a singer, you must be extremely cautious not to emulate effects like this at least until you have learned what balance feels like in your own voice.

What Mike realized was that he had been making the wrong song choices in the beginning of his development. Aggressive song choices such as the songs by the rock star above can be disastrous for a strainer.

And the reason Mike's bandmates were successful night after night? They weren't modeling their voices after a notoriously strained singer who could do nothing but yell - they knew they had to find balance in order to survive the rigors of touring. I know this because I worked with them to improve their sense of balance too.

After making that discovery, we began to find rock songs for Mike that were still challenging and enjoyable to sing, but were by singers who sang into their higher ranges with ease, rather than with a great deal of strain, as with his previous influences. While I would not deny Mike the chance to explore the extreme vocal style he is fascinated by in the future, doing that experimenting before his voice is free enough to do so does not allow his voice to experience ease when singing songs. You should never attempt to push, grind, strain or experiment with extreme styles on your voice before you are able to sing with some degree of balance through your critical bridge between your low and high voice. Since identifying the problem and working on strengthening Mike's voice naturally, Mike's vocal development has made great improvements.

The goal of finding the right song, at least in the beginning of your development, is to find songs that enable your voice to flow most easily according to your abilities. Choose your songs based on the components in this chapter, so you can improve most quickly as a vocalist. But first:

Some Guidelines

In order to realize your Singer's Instinct, your voice should have the ability to vocalize over at least the basic vowel and consonant sounds for your voice-habit through your critical bridge.

> "The wind is filled with songs. So many songs, which one is mine? One must be right for me. Which song of all the songs when there's a song for every star. And there are oh, so many stars, so many stars."
>
> - ALAN & MARILYN BERGMAN

Just remember: if you are struggling with most sound combinations, many songs will likely intensify these problems, as the continual vowel and consonant changes and jumps in pitches make most modern songs much more difficult than exercises.

While you don't want to deny yourself the pleasure of singing songs, be careful not to overdo it by straining. Choose songs that support your voice's current strengths rather than working against it with songs that have too many challenges too soon.

Genre

Certain genres like R&B, soul, heavy rock, and musical theatre can be especially demanding for beginning vocalists because of their wide ranges and strong, powerful intensities. While you can try to hold back on your intensity without belting, often the character of the song and lyrics are so built into the song that it's just too hard to resist getting carried away.

Treat these songs as if they were 150 pound weights at the gym - save them for when your coordination is stronger and you've built up enough control. Genres like folk, country, some older jazz, and acoustic rock, can often be much easier to handle for beginning vocalists because of their almost spoken approaches and easy to medium intensities.

Following Influences

As a singer, you are the fruit of the vocalists you have grown up listening to. In the beginning, you should tune into the qualities of songs of singers that feel more familiar to you. It's more important at this point to build confidence through songs that are familiar to you than to move on to songs that may be new to your listening palette. Let the qualities of the singers you've always admired guide you, rather than choosing artists who may be unfamiliar. Just be careful not to copy the bad habits of the singers you admire if you experience strain in doing it.

If your listening background compels you to explore more difficult songs, such as those from R&B, rock, or musical theatre, make sure you follow the vowel tuning guidelines from chapters: Overcoming Your Voice-Habit, and Vocal Power.

Male/Female

For now, at least, we ought to keep things simple: The songs you choose in the beginning should be by an artist the same sex as you. Otherwise, the song will require some advanced tweaking of keys to make it work for your voice.

Level of Difficulty

Make sure you choose a song that is appropriate for your current ability. The melodic and rhythmic aspects of the melody shouldn't be any more difficult than you can comfortably handle, at least at the beginning of your singing journey.

Note Range: Your song should be within a range that is comfortable for you now, but provides a few small challenges.

Medium Intensity/Volume: The song should be an easy dynamic, that is, not too hard or intense and not too soft or breathy sounding.

> "The fatal mistake is that unripe artists undertake the most difficult tasks before possessing the necessary ability."
>
> - GIOVANNI LAMPERTI

Your Relationship to the Lyric: You should be interested in the song and be able to connect with it musically, intellectually, emotionally, or in all of these ways!

Age/Experience: In relation to the last point, the song you choose should ideally be age appropriate. If you're a young teenager, you may want to avoid singing songs about a divorce.

Do Your Song Research

By exploring iTunes, Youtube, and some other great websites like musicovery.com, you can start to find other music that you may not have known about just by exploring the songs and artists you already enjoy. Keep a small notebook on you, and keep a tally of songs that occur to you throughout the day, so you can always refer back to them. Create a list of 60 or more songs that you really enjoy. Then, over time, work that list down to five to ten songs that you want to focus on and learn from over the next few months. Keep an eye for songs that feel particularly comfortable and that really turn on your Singer's Instinct. Note the characteristics and elements of those songs that make them particularly great for your voice, and try to find more just like them!

Choosing the Right Key

This can be tricky. You may sometimes find that the key of a song is difficult not only because of the low or high notes, but also because certain notes of the song, sometimes very important ones, land in awkward places of the voice, such as a bridge. Sometimes the problem can be dealt with by making a few adjustments to the vowel, but at other times changing the key even just one or two notches up or down will shift key notes out of problem areas and provide a much easier and more enjoyable singing experience.

It's important as a singer to have a way of transposing songs to fit your voice as you need it, if possible. You might want to invest in a computer program that can alter the keys of songs for you. Amazing Slow Downer is a great one that can adjust both the key and the speed of the song, should you also need to slow it down to better hear a complicated line. It also allows you to loop certain sections of songs should you want to study more closely particular moments of the song.

EXERCISES

1) What are some artists and song ideas that you can explore further that are relevant for your voice-habit and skill-level?

_____, _____

_____, _____

_____, _____

_____, _____

2) Who are your influences as a singer? Who did you grow up with?

_____

_____

_____

3) What style of music are you most familiar with? What type of musical personality or types of songs come most easily to you, do you feel most comfortable with?

_____

4) What are your unique limitations and strengths <u>at this time</u>?

_____

_____

18. FINDING THE RIGHT TEACHER

Goals: Find a voice teacher who can help you use your voice effectively.

Why? Voice teachers are not required to have been trained in the complex art of voice teaching. By finding a teacher who is trained to equip you in coordinating a balanced voice, you will develop much more range, ease, and power, efficiently reaching your goals faster.

. . . .

When I went looking for a voice teacher after I moved to London, UK, many years ago, I knew I had to find a good one to keep me on track. I had always relied on the method I had been taught at university in Canada, but thought I might check out some new approaches. I did quite a thorough search, including seriously considering studying with the former coach of a singer I really looked up to. But ultimately, I realized that virtually all of the coaches I had looked at did not use an established system for dealing with the rigors of contemporary singing - and it seemed the singer I looked up to had left a trail of visits to other teachers as well. So I decided to work with a teacher I knew I could rely on - the only teacher at the time who taught the method I had been learning. The decision was a wise one, allowing continuity with a system that had already been giving me results that I trusted.

Likewise, you need to be able to find a teacher you can completely trust to guide your voice to a better place. To accomplish both the right tune up for your voice and to develop your voice to its fullest potential, you need to be sure that the voice training you pursue is credible and efficient in identifying and counterbalancing your unique vocal issues for contemporary singing. The unfortunate reality of modern voice training is that most teachers are not trained in this manner.

Do not select a voice teacher with few credentials because they are cheap. If you can, find an instructor who is rigorously trained in assessing and balancing the full spectrum of voices - a skill extremely rare considering most teachers are only trained to sing, not teach.

The majority of voice teachers today are not trained, and are not required by anyone to be trained in assessing and prescribing appropriate vocal solutions to the variety of voice-conditions that singers for modern music encounter. That is, voice teachers are most often not trained specifically to help you to stay balanced from one part of your voice to another without breaking or straining.

Certain overly simple advice is common within the voice teaching community, as many teachers often try and create the desired vocal effects in a singer by describing the outcome, rather than working on the development of the internal mechanism to achieve it. Remember that the solutions to vocal problems are best applied through cause and effect: direct and precise changes to airflow, vocal cord function, or vowel tuning adjustments.

Developed singers may experience strong sensations of resonance or increased breath pressure through support, but because the singing experience is so subjective and different from singer to singer, explaining the sensations of these end results is not a reliable tool for creating these sensations in others. Instead, it simply describes one person's subjective sensation. Although some things can be learned by hearing about another's experience, in the end these sensations are merely experiences that some (and not others) may feel as the result of a healthy and free functioning voice.

Hoping to get other singers to experience the same sensations as the one instructing via descriptions typically does not create the right balance for those sensations to actually occur in a healthy, sustainable way - particularly in challenging areas of the voice. A vague, idealistic discussion and a loose attempt at throat visualizations may seem to provide some kind of shift to the airflow, muscular and/or resonant coordinations, and thus the tonal quality. The problem is, how can one measure with any accuracy which variable is being adjusted and exactly how it is being adjusted, especially considering that the voice requires such precise and deliberate changes in difficult areas? It is challenging to achieve any consistency or balance through such hopeful shots in the dark. If, however, you find that certain visualization techniques are helpful to your practice, then keep applying them. Just remember that attempting to adjust the voice by anything other than developing the correct muscles and habits that underlie the effects these visualizations describe will often create inaccurate changes, unnecessary added pressure, unnecessary and over-exerting muscular effort, over-manipulation of words, and other imbalances that are ultimately limiting to the voice. Ideally, your teacher should know how to create a condition of balance in your voice rather than just talk about how that balance should feel. Find the right teacher!

Questions To Ask Your Prospective Teacher

1. What skills have they developed as a vocalist? They should have an ability to sing through their critical bridge relatively easily, without straining or suddenly creating a breathy tone, so they can demonstrate how a balanced coordination should sound to you.

2. What training have they received as a vocalist? Are their voice teachers recognized experts in the vocal community? Have they learned from a variety of teachers or just one or two? How long have they studied voice for?

3. Are they still studying with a teacher or contributing to a vocal community? If so, who? The best teacher is a student who is still learning. Learning singing is a lifelong journey, not just something you study for a few years at university. All teachers should be intrinsically motivated to continue to seek out training to keep them up to date with new advancements, and to keep them in touch with the learning process.

4. What skills have they developed as a voice teacher? Just because they are successful singers doesn't mean they have been trained to teach singing. Voice teaching is a very complex skill that requires significant training. Ask what their systems are for assessing voices, how they determine what kind of help you need, and what exercises they prescribe to balance your voice. Do they merely describe how singing correctly should feel, or do they have specific exercises that create that condition for you?

5. Have they ever been or are they accredited by an organization that oversees voice teachers? Find out what organization they are affiliated with and if that organization has a history of assisting singers for the kind of music you are looking to learn, what the requirements for membership are, and if they are required to demonstrate their expertise to be a member. If they no longer carry an affiliation, find out why.

6. What styles of music are they comfortable teaching? Your teacher should have a good grasp of a reliable singing technique that is useful for modern music as well as how to teach it, although they may not necessarily be able to teach every style of music. That's okay. Style can be learned from studying other singers within that genre. You can't do that, however, without having learned a useful vocal technique that can be applied to that style. So be careful your teacher is able to teach you technique that is ultimately applicable to the style of music you want to learn.

7. Most importantly, how do they teach? What does a typical lesson consist of? Do they rely strictly on subjective advice of their experiences as singers such as breath support, tone placement, or visualizations? Or do they use cause and effect solutions that are readily applied to voices different than their own?

8. Do you gel with their personality? A good teacher/student partnership is one that feels right, comfortable and can be trusting.

19. Vocal Health

> **Goal:** Understand how to support the free function of your voice by maintaining optimum health.
>
> **Why?** A healthy voice requires the much more challenging maintenance of the prime condition of your body in its entirety.

. . . .

In order to sing your best, it's important to make sure your vocal apparatus is and remains as healthy as possible. This chapter provides you with some things to remain aware of on your journey to unleash your Singer's Instinct. After all, the voice is a very sensitive instrument - anything you eat, drink, think, or feel can affect it. Because of its fragile and changing nature, maintaining an optimal voice can be challenging, but it is crucial to your basic vocal abilities and creativity.

Optimal Hydration

You may have guessed how important it is to drink water. A typical person should drink 8 - 12 glasses of water a day! To discover your optimal hydration requirements, take your weight in pounds and divide it in half. That's how many ounces of water you should be drinking every day.

Don't fall into the trap of thinking that drinking water when you sing will keep your vocal cords moist. It's not true! Remember, liquids pass over your larynx and into your stomach - never going anywhere close to your vocal cords. And thank your lucky stars it doesn't: If it did, you would be in great physical danger since the sensitive tissues of the larynx and lungs are only designed for airflow, not liquids or food.

The only way to keep your vocal cords hydrated is to make sure your whole body is hydrated. Don't think chugging a liter in the middle of the afternoon will do the trick - it won't! You'll just empty it out in the bathroom half an hour later. You must be continually sipping throughout the day so your body has a chance to fully absorb the moisture, so that it can eventually get to your vocal cords - crucial for keeping your voice in top condition.

Where You Need It Most

Your vocal cords, larynx, and resonating chambers are some of the least important vital systems of your body. So whenever your health begins to waver, whether it be from allergies, lack of sleep, or a hard night of partying, resources like hydration, which you need to keep your cords moist, will be diverted away to take care of what's causing you ill-health elsewhere. Great for survival, but terrible for singing. Make sure you take care of yourself.

Dehydrating Fluids

Minimize or avoid fluids that can dehydrate you - especially caffeine and alcohol. These can dry out the vocal cords causing them to swell and become puffy. They can make your voice sound husky and limit the free vibration of your vocal cords. If you drink caffeine and/or alcohol, you should drink the equivalent in water PLUS your daily 8 - 12 glasses. And even that isn't guaranteed to rebalance your hydration levels or vocal health.

Rest

Next to hydration, at the top of your list for vocal health should be sleep and vocal rest! Like any muscles, your vocal cords needs rest. Make sure you get enough by getting your minimum amount of rest every night, and take one day off singing every week where you can rest your voice completely. You need it to fully restore and repair wear and tear. Also, you need your full concentration when singing and that's impossible if you're tired.

Whispering

Many singers are surprised to learn that whispering can be almost as damaging to your voice as shouting. If you need vocal rest, rest your voice completely and don't speak at all. If you must speak, speak normally. Excessive air against the vocal cords as you whisper can only create more problems by irritating the delicate vocal cords.

Speaking

Some people develop the habit of speaking near the very bottom of their range engaging only the TA muscles and pulls the vocal cord out of a healthy antagonistic balance with the CT muscles. It also pulls out crucial energetic higher overtones in your voice, which means your voice won't get the acoustic feedback it needs to work easily and efficiently. If you feel you are speaking too low, speak a few notes higher in your range at a more optimum speaking pitch. You shouldn't hear any distortion or feel any strain, although you may feel silly at first. Just remember your listener is not necessarily going to hear the differences you feel - they will just hear a freer, more vibrant voice.

Medication

Make sure you understand the effects of any medication you are taking on your vocal health. Medications for allergies can be particularly problematic as they can create swelling within the vocal cords themselves. There are a few effective alternative options for medications these days, so you may or may not be able to minimize the impact on your voice through an alternative. Just let your doctor know that the maintenance of your singing voice is a concern.

Clearing Your Throat

If you are clearing your throat a lot, the most important thing to consider is why you feel the need to clear your throat to begin with. Is there something in your diet that needs to be changed? Is there something not quite right with the way you speak? If you feel the need to clear your throat when you sing, is there something wrong with your singing technique? Make sure you work out what the problem is so you can find the right solution.

If your throat is feeling irritated, try putting your head over some warm steam and inhale (but be careful with hot water!). Warm steam can be very therapeutic for the voice. Ensure you are taking in plenty of fluids (that are not caffeinated or alcoholic) to make it easier to loosen phlegm.

Smoking

When you smoke, the fumes you ingest repeatedly burn the vocal cords and the inner tissues of your mouth, throat and lungs before toxifying the bloodstream. The chemicals and smoke pass repeatedly and directly over your delicate cords making you sound husky, and putting them and everything else at risk for a wide array of life-threatening diseases. Marijuana is especially problematic as the filters that are typically used in smoking it are less effective than filters for  conventional cigarettes and can potentially do even more damage.

Acid Reflux

If you experience regular heartburn, or if you find yourself waking up in the morning with a husky voice, talk to your doctor about whether or not you are experiencing acid reflux. This causes acid buildup from your stomach to reverse back up through your esophagus (your food pipe) and spill over into your larynx, burning the outer layers of your vocal cords. This can ruin any chances of getting a clean sound, and can be permanently damaging.

Make sure you minimize or eliminate caffeine, alcohol, spicy or acidic foods, and especially limit eating for three - four hours before you sleep to avoid reflux in the middle of the night. Also, you may want to consider propping the head of your bed up a few inches if you experience persistent problems.

Technique Versus Style

Unlike any other instrument, you only have one pair of vocal cords - they can never be replaced. As celebrity vocal coach Dave Stroud says, it's important to learn the difference between singing with good vocal technique (a healthy way of singing that will ensure your vocal longevity) and creative vocal style.

Style usually pushes the boundaries of vocal technique and can potentially damage the voice if you are not careful. Although vocal style can help you stand out as a singer, not taking care with your vocal technique can dramatically limit how freely and expressively you are able to experiment with vocal style, or use your voice at all, especially in the long term. Singing with bad vocal technique can permanently damage

> "The key to vocal health and stamina comes down to the physical process one is using when they practice or perform. Keeping a balance between the sub-glottal pressure and the amount of closed quotient (within the vocal cord closure) is very important. The difficulty within this lies in the ability to continue to be unique and creative as an artist and maintain as much vocal balance as possible."
>
> - DAVE STROUD

your voice and quickly end any career or enjoyment of singing.

So, while it's tempting to develop only your vocal styling as an aspiring singer, you will find yourself becoming easily limited and frustrated when your voice becomes jammed or strained, or is not available to you in the way you need it. You must learn how to use your voice in an efficient way. That is, you must maintain a healthy and expressive voice free of strain and clutter over the widest range and dynamic as possible.

EXERCISES

1) Roughly how many glass of water do you typically drink in a day? Is this enough? What can you do to get your intake up?

_____

2) What dietary components should you be aware of that might be causing you harm?

_____

3) What health concerns have you noticed that might interfere with your laryngeal and overall vocal health?

_____

20. Voice Training Myths

Goals: Identify inefficient or dangerous voice training practices.

Why? By identifying common myths about voice training you can save yourself from ill-informed techniques that can adversely affect your ability to access your natural voice.

. . . .

When you are developing the voice for singing, you have to make small, deliberate, and precise changes in order to be effective. The tools in this book should have introduced you to these skills, allowing you to sing with more range, better diction, fuller breathing and an overall natural quality.

But what to make, then, of the array of other voice training advice such as diction, breathing, imagery, or "voice placement"? While these things can offer some enhancements, they do not and cannot address with any precision the core challenges at the root of nearly every singer's problems - transitioning through your critical bridge. They do not teach you how to make the precise adjustments required to create a condition of balance between all the elements in your voice to sing in an even voice with range, ease, and strength. If, however, you feel inspired to pursue other methodologies, be cautious about going in hot pursuit of skills that might not be beneficial to your current voice-habit or skill level.

Always remember what your ultimate goal is and the most direct way to get there, and be cautious about methodologies that use the following myths as their foundation. The techniques outlined in this book go much beyond these methodologies, creating actual changes of balance in the voice with much greater precision.

The Myth of Support as the Singer's Solution

Your tiny vocal cords are no match for the powerful blast of air pressure that it is possible for your abdomen muscles to produce. Because of their miniature nature, they need very little air in order to vibrate freely, easily, and efficiently. The air pressure from your lungs is capable of 200 watts, but the vocal cords can only withstand

roughly two watts of power before they become overwhelmed, tighten and/or tire out. That means that your lungs can produce more than 100 times the power your vocal cords can actually handle! No wonder we strain our vocal cords so easily!

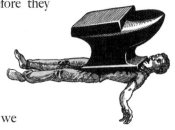

Less Is More

When in difficulty, use less air; rarely should you use more. Training advice such as blasting more air or applying more breath pressure can potentially be ruinous for voices, especially if you are already using too much. Without an understanding of how to engage your voice - across your entire range and on all vowels - in a correct balance between your vocal cords and the breath pressure

> **"Sing on an indispensable minimum of breath; the least amount of air you can use, but no less."**
>
> - EDGAR F. HERBERT-CAESARI

that activates them, excessive breath pressure can be disastrous, leaving you no chance of reaching your potential, or even of singing safely.

You need very little air to sing efficiently. The vocal cords should never tighten from excessive airflow. If your vocal cords can't handle all the air pressure you send to them, you can bet they will enlist the aid of other extrinsic muscles to try and withstand the air pressure for them. This is exactly what you want to avoid. In this way you will never truly develop your vocal cords to strengthen properly. Worse, you put your vocal cords at risk for a variety of serious vocal problems, including swelling and developing nodules that can permanently damage your voice.

Use as little air as possible to get the strongest vocal sound you can. If you train in this way, your vocal strength will develop gradually and easily over time.

Putting Breath Support into Perspective

If relaxing, visualizing, breathing and adding breath pressure was all you needed to be able to do to develop the voice, all martial arts enthusiasts would, by definition, be great singers. But of course that's not the case. The vocal cords must be coordinated to handle the air you send them via the right, continually changing balance between the vocal cords and optimal vowel formation. Doing breathing exercises and adding more support can increase the feeling of well-being in the singer. However, it most likely will fall short of teaching them how to shift between the low and high parts of their voices correctly, especially if their vocal cords have not been properly developed to withstand air pressure in those parts of the voice.

> "There is no correct breath support without correct phonation. You cannot support the voice correctly unless you have a correct balance in your voice's resonance."
>
> - GIOACCHINO LAURO LI VIGNI

In a well developed voice, the air pressure from the abdomen sends into vibration the vocal cords as they close exactly just enough for the pitch and intensity required by the singer. Since a well balanced singer will feel her vocal cords very little (only a singer singing with difficulty will feel tension in the throat), the sensation of this air pressure is perhaps the strongest sensation she may feel aside from the strong sensations of resonance. More importantly, breathing is the only part of the entire singing mechanism you can actually see (without medical instruments it's nearly impossible to see the vocal cords or the resonance they produce).

TECHNICAL SUPPORT

In time, as your vocal cords become better coordinated to resist only the appropriate amount of breath pressure, your body will naturally, by default, easily create the correct amount of breath pressure support that the vocal cords require. When you have a balance between the expelled air and the correct amount of closure with your vocal cords, you will experience more natural sensations of support.

Support can only be experienced in an already well-balanced voice that has a balanced critical bridge. A singer who does not have their critical bridge tuned up will experience varying degrees of vocal cord strain and shouldn't try to create a feeling of support to assist with these issues. Adding any kind of extrinsic musculature and/or breath pressure to your singing to aid in relieving strain is counter-productive and can be viciously damaging, leading to problems plaguing singers everywhere.

The Myth of Breathing Techniques

While it is important to have a low breath for singing, if the vocal cords and coordination of your larynx are not yet developed, any further instruction in breathing is going to help your singing only peripherally at best. Instead, be deliberate about how hard or soft your vocal cords are closing, how much or how little air you are using, and the optimal vowel-tunings. As stated in earlier chapters, these three elements are the only ways to manifest controlled changes in the voice.

The Myth of Voice Placement

Every singer, including well-developed ones, experiences the sensations their voice produces in different, very subjective ways. That's ok! Strong feelings of resonance and a strong voice will come as your voice gains balance. But trying to prematurely force a feeling of resonance, or to "place the voice" somewhere, without adjusting vowel formation or before the vocal cords or larynx are equipped to do so, can only create more problems. Many singers who try using voice placement techniques end up sounding nasal or forced. Forcing anything in your voice always creates inappropriate tension of some kind that can be very damaging in the long term.

The Myth of Smiling for High Notes

I've heard some vocal coaches and choral directors encouraging their singers to smile when singing high notes. While this does help to engage some higher sounding resonances, it also has a tendency to cause discomfort in the throat by creating a raised larynx (voice-box), over-stretching the vocal cords and creating vocal problems if not used with caution. There's nothing wrong with smiling as an expression of what you're feeling in the music. As a vocal technique to help you sing high notes, however, it can be very dangerous.

The Myth of Coating Your Throat

I've often been asked what you can drink if your vocal cords are feeling dry or irritated. Some have asked about lozenges, throat sprays, tea, gargles - I've even heard of a singer who had been advised to drink olive oil before they went onstage!

To understand why these don't work, we just need to briefly refer to our chapter on basic voice physiology. Your "air pipe" where your vocal cords are and your "food pipe" which all liquids and foods pass through are two entirely different mechanisms in your body. Your air pipe and your vocal cords within them are only designed for airflow - nothing else. This means that it is impossible for any products to provide direct relief to your vocal cords - aside from perhaps coating, albeit briefly, the inside or back of your mouth. If you wish to get more hydration to the vocal cords themselves, you will have to provide your body with optimal hydration. Refer to the previous chapter on vocal health for more details.

Remember these basic rules as you explore the world of voice and it will greatly simplify your training, save you time, and make your learning process much more enjoyable.

EXERCISES

1) Listen to a few songs of two or three singers you admire the most.
What is their use of their vocal cords like? Are they breathy-toned?
Gentle? Strained? Balanced? Do they apply too much breath
pressure? If so, can you hear how their vocal cords react by
tightening?

_____

_____

2) What techniques have you been taught in the past? How can you
adapt them with what you have learned about vocal balance through
addressing and training your voice-habit?

_____

_____

_____

GLOSSARY

Beat Accents: The beats that carry the strongest accent of the rhythmic cycle of a song.

Belting: An advanced vocal technique that produces a very powerful sound in the upper part of the vocal range.

Breath Support: The engagement of the abdominal muscles against the lungs during exhalation. When the vocal cords work correctly, closing and resisting the column of air from the breath, it sends them into vibration, giving the experience of feeling supported by the airflow.

Bridge (voice): A range of about three notes where a transition occurs between the muscle coordination and dominant amplifying sensations of the registers above and below these notes.

Bridge (song): Unlike verses, choruses, and pre-choruses, the bridge usually only occurs once in a song in order to give it variety and contract, a break from the familiar repeating structures of the verse and chorus.

Chest Voice/Chest Register: An area of the vocal range where many singers experience their chest resonating much more than in the head voice, where less chest resonance is experienced.

Chords: A group of 2 or more notes sounded together or in sequence with a harmonic relationship. Most chords use at least three notes.

Chord Structure: The series of chords played within a song.

Chord Progression: (see chord structure)

Common Time: A time signature indicating 4/4 time, or four quarter notes to very bar.

Consonance: Intervals and chords in music are termed either consonant or dissonant. Consonance is the perceived quality of a musical sound that is pleasant and stable-sounding, not requiring resolution to another note or chord.

Core Challenge: The difficulty of singing from the low voice (chest/ upper chest) into the high voice (middle/head) via the critical bridge.

Critical Bridge: The most important bridge in the voice where it makes its biggest change between the low and high voice. It is the only bridge, according to recent modern research, where both the muscles and amplifying space change or transition entirely. It is the one area where most singers are challenged to some degree, and problems in this area if left unchecked can create a host of vocal problems.

Diphthongs: Diphthongs are two adjacent vowel sounds that "slide" from one to the other in the same syllable. For example, in the word "buy" ("AH" + "EE").

Dissonance: A note, interval or chord that suggests unrelieved tension, creating a "pull" towards a more stable note or chord.

Dotted Notes: A dot alongside a note that increases the total value of the note by half its original value.

Downbeat: The first beat in a bar of music, which marks the beginning of each bar "cycle". It's name comes from the downward stroke of the orchestra conductor at the beginning of every bar. It sometimes carries the strongest rhythmic accent, although in modern music it is just as often implied or unaccented.

Dynamics: Degrees of softness or loudness in volume.

Embellishments: A note or series of notes not necessary to the melody but that enhance it with musical flourishes or ornamentation. Sometimes embellishments are written in the music by the composer, at other times they express the singer's own creativity.

Falsetto: A vocal coordination where only the outer edges of the vocal cords close, losing their ability to stay closed with more fullness in the upper voice, creating a rush of air and a peculiar sound.

Head Voice/Head Register: An area of the vocal range where many singers experience their head resonating more in contrast to the low voice (chest), where little head resonance is experienced.

Interval: The difference in pitch between two notes.

Intonation: The ability to play/sing in tune.

Keeping Time: The ability to remain aware of where you are in the rhythmic cycles of the music.

Key: A relationship of notes and chords based on and centered around the first note of a scale.

Key Signature: The number of sharps or flats at the beginning of a song's musical notation that indicate the song's key.

Licks: (see embellishments)

Melodic Contour: The ranges of high and low points in a melody that give the melody a particular shape and quality over time.

Melody: A sequence of single tones varying in pitch and duration. They are often based on a few short phrases, or recurring motifs.

Middle C: The halfway point on the piano/keyboard, also designated as "C4", representing the fourth C key from the bottom. In musical notation, it is notated on the first ledger line beneath treble clef, or the first ledger line above the bass clef.

Middle Voice/Middle Register: A range of a few notes in a voice where many singers experience the sensations of the low and high voice overlapping in almost equal proportion.

Musical Notation: A system of musical symbols used by musicians and singers to play/sing the music as set out by the composer.

Musical Staff: A set of horizontal lines and spaces where a sequence of notes is notated both on and between the lines.

Octave: A musical interval of 12 half-steps or semi tones, or a span of 7 unique notes (where the eighth repeats the first note an octave higher) in the diatonic scale.

Pentatonic Scale: Five tones, usually the first, second, third, fifth, and sixth degrees of the major diatonic scale.

Phrasing: The style in which a group of notes or a section of a melody is played or sung. Phrasing can be written into the music's notation or can be a choice in the way it is performed.

Pre-Chorus: An optional section of a song that occurs after the verse, but just before the chorus, creating a transition from one to the other.

Quarter Note: A common note value used in music equal to two eighth notes.

Register: An area of the voice where many singers feel a range of notes function and resonate in a similar way.

Repeat Bar: A musical symbol used in notation that has a thick bar line with two dots in the middle spaces of the ledger line, that indicate the bars between them must be played at least twice as indicated in the music.

Repeat Bar: A symbol on the musical staff of parallel thick and thin bar lines with two dots on the middle spaces of the staff, indicating the passages between them should be played twice, or more.

Rest: An interval of silence in music the length of which is indicated by the symbol.

Riffs: (see embellishments)

Scale: A sequence of notes with potentially varied ascending or descending schemes. For the purposes of singing, scales are used to help make certain technique concepts easier to produce in the voice.

Swing: Commonly a subdivision of two eighth beats where the first eighth is played slightly longer than the second, which is slightly shortened.

Syncopation: An unexpected variation to some aspect of the rhythm.

Tempo: The speed at which a song is played, usually indicated in bpm (beats per minute).

Time Signature: A symbol at the beginning of the musical staff indicating how to count the music. The first number indicates how many beats are in a bar, while the second number indicates the length of each beat. In 4/4 time, for example, there are four quarter notes to every bar.

Tonal Center: The tonic, or first degree, of the song's key, which the music essentially revolves around. It has the most stability in the melody and chord structure, imbuing the note with a sense of being "home".

Tone: A specific pitch, an interval equal to two semitones or half steps, or the overall quality of sound.

Tonic: (see tonal center)

Trill: A musical embellishment that consists of a fast alternation between a principal note and a counterpart a whole or half step away.

Tune up: adjustments made to create functionality at peak efficiency. In singing, each vowel sound requires separate tuning in every area of the voice, particularly in higher ranges.

Vibrato: In singing, an oscillation produced by slight fluctuations of air pressure and pitch.

Vocal Cords: Two small bands of muscle and tissue (or folds) that extend from the sides of the larynx. They vibrate when pulled together by the singer, resisting airflow from the lungs, creating a basic pitch and tone.

Vocal Range: The measure of pitches over which the voice can sing.

Vocal Resonance: The process by which the sound from the vocal cords is amplified in intensity and enhanced in timbre through the cavities above the larynx.

Vocal Technique: The fundamentals of healthy singing and vocal development.

Voice-Habit: A condition that a singer tends to get trapped in. A singer's voice-habit is alone responsible for nearly all a singer's problems including loss of: range, strength, balance, endurance, health, and general efficiency.

Voice Placement: A classical singing concept intended to create a particular sound production in the singer.

SOURCES

Tracing The Instinct

Kimpel, Dan. "One Of The Media's Foremost Authorities On Popular
     Music." Interview by Brandon Brophy. The Singer's Edge. 16
     Oct. 2007. Web.
The American Heritage® Dictionary of the English Language, Fourth
     Edition, ©2000 by Houghton Mifflin Company. Updated in
     2009. Published by Houghton Mifflin Company.

The Vocal Impulse

Barbereux-Parry, M. Vocal Resonance: Its Source and Command.
     North Quincy, MA: Christopher Pub. House, 1979. Print.
Brown, Oren. Discover Your Voice: How to Develop Healthy Voice
     Habits. San Diego: Singular Pub. Group, 1996. Print.
Henny, John. Personal Conversations. 2010. Print.
Herbert-Caesari, Edgar F. The Science and Sensations of Vocal Tone;
     a School of Natural Vocal Mechanics. Boston: Crescendo,
     1968. Print.
Herbert-Caesari, Edgar F. The Voice of the Mind. Boston: Crescendo,
     1963. Print.
Miller, Donald Gray. Resonance in Singing: Voice Building through
     Acoustic Feedback. Princeton, NJ: Inside View, 2008. Print.
Miller, Richard. The Structure of Singing. New York: Oxford UP,
     1996. Print.
Music Genre List. Accessed May 28, 2012. http://musicgenreslist.com/.
Niziolek, Carrie. "Vocal Registers: Acoustic and Physiological Analysis
     of Voice Quality in Singing." Massachusetts Institute of
     Technology. Last modified 18 May 2006. Accessed 13 Aug.
     2012. http://web.mit.edu/carrien/Public/6.541/voice-
     carrien.pdf.
Reid, Cornelius L. The Free Voice: a Guide to Natural Singing. New
     York: Joseph Patelson Music House, 1972. Print.

Riggs, Seth. "Vocal Instructor to the Stars." Singer's Edge, Episode 6 (February 2008). July 15, 2011. http://itunes.apple.com/ca/podcast/singing-singers-edge-talk/id270023086.

Stark, James Arthur. Bel Canto: A History of Vocal Pedagogy. Toronto: University of Toronto, 2003. Print.

Stroud, Dave. Speech Level Singing Certified Instructor Manual. Internal publication, 2008.

Titze, Ingo R. Principles of Voice Production. Englewood Cliffs, NJ: Prentice Hall, 1994. Print.

Titze, Ingo R. and Katherine Abbott.Vocology: The Science and Practice of Voice Habilitation. Salt Lake City, Utah: National Center for Voice and Speech, 2012. Print.

"Larynx superior view." Empowher. Web. 15 July 2011. http://www.empowher.com/files/ebsco/images/si1393.jpg.

The Musical Impulse

Ear Training. Auralia. Accessed 15 July 2011. http://www.risingsoftware.com/auralia/.

EarMaster. Web. 15 July 2011. <http://www.earmaster.com>.

Furstner, Michael. "Basic Rhythms." Jazz Class. Accessed 15 June 2011. http://www.jazclass.aust.com/rhythmcl/rc03.htm.

Good Ear. Accessed 15 Aug. 2011. http://www.good-ear.com.

Lindsay, Kenneth A. and Nordquist, Peter R. "A Technical Look at Swing Rhythm in Music." Southern Oregon University. Accessed August 27, 2012. http://www.tlafx.com/jasa06_ig.pdf

Sing & See. Accessed 15 July 2011. http://www.singandsee.com.

Wheatley, Margaret J. and Myron Kellner-Rogers. A Simpler Way. San Francisco: Berrett-Koehler, 1996. Print.

"Christmas Rhythms." Layton Music. Accessed 15 June 2011. http://laytonmusic.wordpress.com/2007/12/21/christmas-rhythms/.

"Vibrato Speed." Sonic Transfer. Accessed 15 July 2011. http://sonictransfer.com/vibrato-electronic-music-production-tutorial.shtml.

The Vocal Personality Impulse

Jazz. Dir. Ken Burns. By Ken Burns. Perf. Wynton Marsalis. PBS, 2001. DVD.

Marantz Henig, Robin. "Play Kids." Taking Play Seriously. The New York times. Accessed 15 June 2011. http://www.nytimes.com/2008/02/17/magazine/17play.html.

Nichtern, David. David Nichtern. Last modified 19 Jan. 2010. Accessed 15 August 2011. http://www.davidnichtern.com.

"Pentatonic Scale Structure." Your Personal Singing Guide. Accessed 15 July 2011. http://www.your-personal-singing-guide.com/pentatonic-scale.html

"Song Structure." Ethan Hein. Accessed 15 July 2011. http://www.ethanhein.com/theory/rhythm_notation.html.

Wheatley, Margaret J. and Myron Kellner-Rogers. A Simpler Way. San Francisco: Berrett-Koehler, 1996. Print.

Schotz, Susanne. "Linguistic & Paralinguistic Phonetic Variation in Speaker Recognition & Text-to-Speech Synthesis." Department of Linguistics and Phonetics, Lund University. 2002. Accessed August 27, 2012. http://www.speech.kth.se/~rolf/gslt_papers/SusanneSchotz.pdf.

The Impulse of Wise Practice

Brodnitz, Friedrich S. Keep Your Voice Healthy: a Guide to the Intelligent Use and Care of the Speaking and Singing Voice. Boston: Little, Brown, 1988. Print.

Coyle, Daniel. The Talent Code: Greatness Isn't Born: It's Grown, Here's How. New York: Bantam Books, 2009.

Gerson, Ruth . "Ruth Gerson: Interview With Star Vocal Coach, David Stroud." The Huffington Post. Accessed August 28, 2012. http://www.huffingtonpost.com/ruth-gerson/interview-with-star-vocal_b_1186317.html.

Herbert-Caesari, Edgar F. The Voice of the Mind. Boston: Crescendo, 1963. Print.

Li Vigni, Gioacchino L. "Principles Of Â Technique." Tenor Talk Blog. Accessed 04 June 2012. http://tenortalkblog.com/principles-of-technique/.

Loeding, Prof. Rosalie. "Vocal Survival Techniques For Singers Who
        Abuse And Overuse Their Voices." Dr. Grossan, the ENT
        On-Line Consultant. Accessed 15 May 2011.

Loeding, Prof. Rosalie. "Vocal Survival Techniques for Singers Who
        Abuse and Overuse Their Voices." Dr. Grossan, the ENT On-
        Line Consultant. Accessed 15 May 2011.

Riggs, Seth, and John D. Carratello. Singing for the Stars: A Complete
        Program for Training Your Voice. Van Nuys, CA: Alfred
        Pub., 1998. Print.

Stark, James Arthur. Bel Canto: a History of Vocal Pedagogy.
        Toronto: University of Toronto, 2003. Print.

Streisand, Barbra, Alan Bergman, and Marilyn Bergman. What
        Matters Most: Barbra Streisand Sings the Lyrics of Alan and
        Marilyn Bergman. Columbia, 2011. CD.

CPSIA information can be obtained at www.ICGtesting.com
Printed in the USA
BVOW10s1109301113

337677BV00005B/22/P

9 780988 094802